SARA,
Book 2

Solomon's Fine Featherless Friends

Other Hay House Titles by Esther and Jerry Hicks

Books, Calendar, and Card Decks

The Amazing Power of Deliberate Intent (also available in Spanish)

Ask and It Is Given (also available in Spanish)

Ask and It Is Given Cards

Ask and It Is Given Perpetual Flip Calendar

The Astonishing Power of Emotions (available in Spanish in 2009)

The Law of Attraction
(will also be available in Spanish in October 2008)

The Law of Attraction Cards (coming in 2008)

Manifest Your Desires (available June 2008)

Money, and the Law of Attraction
(book; 5-CD set—both available March 2008)

Relationships, and the Law of Attraction
(book; 5-CD set—both available September 2008)

Sara, Book 1: Sara Learns the Secret about the <u>Law of Attraction</u>

Sara, Book 3: A Talking Owl Is Worth a Thousand Words!
(available April 2008)

Spirituality, and the Law of Attraction
(book; 5-CD set—both available March 2009)

The Teachings of Abraham Well-Being Cards

Additional CD Programs

The Amazing Power of Deliberate Intent
(Parts I and II: two 4-CD sets)

Ask and It Is Given (Parts I and II: two 4-CD sets)

The Astonishing Power of Emotions (8-CD set)

The Law of Attraction (4-CD set)

Sara, Book 1 (unabridged audio book; 3-CD set)

DVD Programs

The Law of Attraction in Action, Episode 1 (2-DVD set)

The Secret Behind "The Secret"? (Abraham) (2-DVD set)

∽∼∾

All of the above are available at your local bookstore, or may be ordered by visiting:
Hay House USA: www.hayhouse.com®; Hay House Australia: www.hayhouse.com.au;
Hay House UK: www.hayhouse.co.uk; Hay House India: www.hayhouse.co.in

SARA,
Book 2

Solomon's Fine Featherless Friends

Esther and Jerry Hicks

Illustrated by Caroline S. Garrett

HAY HOUSE, INC.
Carlsbad, California • New York City
London • Sydney • New Delhi

Published in the United States by: Hay House, Inc.: www.hayhouse.com
Published in Australia by: Hay House Australia Pty. Ltd.: www.hayhouse.com.au
Published in the United Kingdom by: Hay House UK, Ltd.: www.hayhouse.co.uk
Published in India by: Hay House Publishers India: www.hayhouse.co.in

Illustrations: © 1999 Caroline S. Garrett

Originally published by Abraham-Hicks Publications:
ISBN: 0-9621219-7-5

Library of Congress Control No.: 2006924805

ISBN: 978-1-4019-1159-1

16 15 14 13 12 11 10 9 8
1st edition, October 2007

Printed in the United States of America

CONTENTS

Introduction

There is rarely anything that I read that can cause me to laugh right out loud. But as I've been proofreading this latest *Sara* novel, Esther frequently calls out to me from her office, "What made you laugh?" as I get caught again and again by the intellectual humor of my old friend, Solomon, and Sara's bright new friend, Seth.

Solomon's Fine Featherless Friends is the book that promises to take you on an emotional joyride to heights of understanding and well-being that will repeatedly and forever thrill and delight you.

The fun you will have with Sara and Seth while you discover the pure and practical formula for fulfilling your life's purpose will be an experience you can share with everyone you love. No matter how good you're feeling right now, you'll feel even better once you experience this newest *Sara* book. We guarantee that you will delight in this next giant step in your journey of more joyous becoming.

— Jerry Hicks

CHAPTER 1

Reaching for Happiness

"Seth, your house is on fire!"

"Yeah, right," Seth scoffed, tensing against another barrage of mockery at his expense. The five-mile ride home on the school bus felt like a hundred miles. The teasing always began the very moment he stepped foot on the bus and lasted without letup until he dragged himself off.

It had begun last March on his very first day in this new school, when his family had moved into the old Johnson place up on the hill. The house had been vacant for some time before they moved in. And even though they had now lived in the home for several months, it didn't look much different now than it had when no one was living there. The same raggedy curtains hung in the kitchen window, the only window that had any curtains at all. The wooden floors were rough and worn, and the walls were covered with marks and cracks and nail holes and all kinds of evidence of several short-term tenants who had lived there before.

No one in the family seemed to mind the way the house looked anyway. They hadn't minded the last one either, or the one before that. It was the *land* his parents were most interested in. Land for gardens and milk cows and goats. Land requiring constant, never-ending work. Land that produced little more than enough for the family to survive.

Seth did not sit up. He continued to lie on his back, nestled tightly on the small bus seat with his sweater over his face, pretending to be asleep.

He no longer flinched at Patrick's rubber snake. You can only jump out of your skin so many times over the same dumb trick. Not since the first or second day on the bus had Seth sat on something sharp or wet. With enough experience, you learn to watch where you're sitting and stepping. (Only once did he fall back recklessly on his seat expecting it to hold him, as every bus seat before had done, only to discover—as his seat tipped over backward, crushing the knees of the angry, yelping girls sitting behind him—that his malicious bus-mates had worked the full length of the bus ride to school that morning to unbolt the seat and then had plotted to leave it open and available for Seth's return ride home at the end of the day.)

From fake spiders to real spiders, from puddles of water in his seat to puddles of honey, Seth now believed he had lived to discover the limited and unimaginative arsenal of these silly goons' tricks. And these bus rides, while certainly far from pleasant, no longer produced much real emotion in him at all.

"Seth, your house *is* on fire! Really, Seth, *look!*"

Seth continued to lie on his seat, eyes closed, smiling, enjoying that, for once, it seemed, he had the upper hand of things. He could hear something new in their voices. They really, really wanted something from him that he could now withhold. Maybe things were beginning to turn. Maybe his father had been right and time had made it better.

"Seth!" The bus driver's voice boomed out, "Get up. Your house *is* on fire!"

Seth's heart stopped. He did not hesitate any longer. He sat up and looked up the hillside and saw his home, such as it was, completely engulfed in flames.

The bus driver pulled over to the side of the road and opened the door of the bus. Seth sat frozen, looking out the window at the smoke billowing up. The smoke was so thick he couldn't see how much damage had been done, and he couldn't see anyone around. There was no fire truck rushing to the rescue and no neighbors clamoring to help. Everything around looked pretty much like it always did. The cows continued to graze, the old goat stood tied to the tree, and the chickens scratched in the front yard while the house burned.

Trixie, the oldest and friendliest of the family's three dogs, ran down the hill and crawled under the gate to greet Seth. She licked his fingers and then nuzzled his pocket looking for a treat. But Seth didn't notice her. He stood in a daze watching the house burn.

The bus driver drove off, telling Seth that he would call for help at the next stop, and Seth waved back limply. There was really no point in calling anyone for help. He could see as the wind changed and the smoke moved away that the house had burned completely to the ground. The only thing left standing was a column of bricks that had been a fireplace and chimney. Seth could hear the soft crackle of some timbers still burning and an occasional pop, pop, as a can of something or other exploded in the rubble.

Seth felt odd as he stood watching the remaining smoldering pieces of wood. What he was feeling wasn't sadness—not even a great sense of loss that one would expect in a situation like this—just an odd feeling of emptiness. There was no reason for any real sense of loss because, in truth, not much had actually been lost. He wasn't fearful that any member of his family was trapped inside because his parents were at the vegetable market every Tuesday and Wednesday; and Samuel, his little brother, had been with him on the bus until he got off at Mrs. Whitaker's place to work in her yard. And there was no feeling of loss of valuable possessions because there weren't any of those. There was a library book that had been checked out and not returned, and Seth felt a pang of guilt that now he couldn't return it.

While he couldn't identify it clearly for himself, in this traumatic moment, what Seth was feeling was more a sense of loss that there had been nothing *to* lose. This extreme experience of bad luck was not, by any means, an isolated incident in the Morris family. It seemed that things usually turned out badly, sooner or later.

Seth sat down on the tree stump with his back to the afternoon sun as the long shadow of his silhouette traveled across the front yard almost all the way up to where the house once stood. He wondered why it was taking so long for anyone to respond to the report from the bus driver that the house was on fire. He wished that his parents would come home.

As he sat there feeling empty and lonely, he began to recall the string of bad luck his family had experienced. In his short life, his family had lived in more than two dozen homes, mostly small farms, and most lacking in any of the modern comforts of life; most didn't have indoor plumbing, and some didn't even have electricity. His family moved from farm to farm, growing what they could, eating whatever they could grow or kill, and selling whatever people in various nearby towns would buy in order to purchase things they couldn't grow. His parents, while still quite young, seemed old, and he couldn't remember the last time either of them seemed happy about anything.

It seemed to Seth that he and his younger brother, Samuel, were always in trouble over something. Seth often wondered if the primary source of their trouble was that they wanted to be happy in a world that their parents had decided was *not* happy. It was as if their parents were determined to properly prepare them for the unhappy plight of their future, and the sooner they could get to a morbid dissatisfaction with life, the easier it would be on them. No dreams were ever encouraged, fun was barely tolerated, and nothing frivolous was allowed.

But every now and again circumstances would simply demand it, and the boys—who were boys, after all—acted up while their parents looked on with disapproval.

As the ashes smoldered, Seth stared blankly

into the smoke remembering the last farm. It was, maybe, the worst place they had ever lived. The house wasn't really a house at all but an old barn with no windows and one very big door. The floor was wooden, raised a few inches off the dirt beneath it, and the cracks in the floor were so wide that large rodents had no trouble at all coming and going, and did so frequently. In time, effort was no longer made to control them; the family grew accustomed to seeing them, and they were just part of life.

Since the house, or barn, or whatever you wanted to call it, was the only structure on the property, everything that was seen as valuable was kept inside; even sacks of feed for the animals were stacked along one wall near the big door. One day while no one was at home, the family mule literally kicked down the front door and happily devoured the flour, molasses, and oats. She managed to do so much damage to the doorway and frame that the front end of the house was left sagging and dangerous. And so, the family moved into a tent while repairs to the old barn could be made.

Seth remembered being glad they were out of the smelly old barn and wishing the whole thing would have fallen down. During the night, while they were sleeping in the tent, he got his wish: The building caught fire, no one knows how, and burned quickly to the ground.

Geez, what is it with us and old houses burning down? Seth thought as he sat perched on his stump watching the smoke billowing up. The wind shifted and the smoke from the smoldering rubble surrounded Seth, making his eyes water. He moved out of the smoke and sat down on a log under the big tree at the side of the house and continued to remember his dismal past.

The tent, it had turned out, provided a much less-than-satisfactory haven for the family because Judy, the family's mule, found it even easier than the barn to plunder for oats. In a space of two weeks, she tore the tent down five times and Seth's parents went searching for a new plan. And Judy, important to the farm because she pulled the plow and the wagon, wasn't shot, although Seth's mother had threatened it many times.

That's how Seth and his family ended up living in the cave. Seth and his brother had been aware of the old cave for months. They often went there to escape from the endless chores their parents seemed to think of. There was never a time that any member of the family just sat around, unproductively, to just *be*. That was seen as wasteful as squandering flour, soap, or money. Even water was handled carefully, since it was hauled in a barrel on a wagon behind Judy. No waste was allowed. And no time was wasted.

But the boys had discovered the cave one afternoon

while they were looking for Judy, who was missing again. It was on the back side of the property, close to the field used for planting oats, but not in plain view from the field. You had to know that the cave was there to find it, for tall weeds and bushes completely covered the entrance. Seth and Samuel had kept the cave as a secret, promising each other that, no matter what, it would remain their special haven. They often talked about how lucky they were to have discovered such a neat place to hide out. And while they seldom went to the cave, and hardly ever went together, they both knew it was there, and they both loved *knowing* that it was there.

"You boys ever seen a cave on this land?" Seth's father growled.

Seth's eyes immediately looked down, and he held his breath, hoping that Samuel wouldn't give up their precious secret. He bent down and picked up a nail from the dirt and fiddled with it in his fingers as if it were so important that he couldn't possibly focus on his father's words and do this important thing at the same time.

Samuel was quiet. His eyes darted to Seth's, and Seth tried to be cool.

"Ed Smith says there's an old cave on the back 40 up in the brush at the base of the cliff," his father continued. "He says it's pretty good sized and would make a good shelter. You boys seen it?"

Seth thought about denying that they knew anything about the cave because surely they would be in trouble for keeping such a secret, for it was certainly evidence that they had wasted time. (On the other hand, when their father did find the cave, and it was certain that he would, if they had denied knowing about it and their father found their rock piles and Judy's old, worn saddle blanket that had mysteriously vanished a few weeks back and had provided a rather comfortable resting pad for the boys, along with a variety of magazines and trinkets they had gathered and left there, there would be really big trouble. The kind of trouble Seth had never told anyone about. The kind of trouble he didn't even like to think about.)

"Yeah, we've seen it," Seth said, faking little interest. "It's pretty creepy."

Samuel's body lurched in his surprise that his big brother had given in so easily. He looked at Seth in amazement and then looked down so no one would notice that his eyes were filling up with tears. This secret cave was so very important to both boys. Now the secret was out, and their haven was gone.

"I can show you if you like, but you won't like it. It's dark and stinky. And who knows what kind of animals live back in there."

"I don't care how creepy it is," his father growled. "It'll take weeks to rebuild the house, and the damn mule keeps uprooting the tent. The cave is a good idea. It'll be warmer, we won't get rained on, and it's already built. Where is it?"

"You wanna go now?" Seth questioned, inwardly trembling in fear. He needed some time to get out there and hide the telling evidence of just how involved in this cave they had actually been.

"There's no time like the present," his father said, taking a long drink of water from the barrel with the dipper and wiping his face on his sleeve. "Let's go."

Seth and Samuel looked at each other and then followed behind their father. *I am going to die,* Seth thought as he followed. His knees felt weak, and he felt sick to his stomach. His mind was racing. *What am I going to do?*

A truck came skidding to a stop down by the gate, and an angry farmer laid heavily on the horn. He stood out on the running board and shouted up the hillside at Seth's father, "Your damn bull has tore up my fence again! I've told you, I'd just as soon shoot the damn thing as look at it. You better get him out of my pasture, *now!* And I want that fence fixed, too!"

Seth's eyes danced and his heart began to sing. That "damn bull," as his neighbor had called him, had pretty much just saved Seth's life.

Seth's father stopped where he was, said something under his breath, and then headed for the tool shed for bailing wire and tools.

"I'll go with you," Seth chirped.

"What are you so happy about?" his father growled.

"Nothin'," Seth said. "Nothin'."

CHAPTER 2

Moving On Again

Seth heard truck doors slam, and it jolted him back into the present. He looked at what had been the house, now just a smoldering pile of rubble. It was amazing how little time it took for an entire house to burn to the ground.

Seth heard his mother's gasp, and then he heard something he couldn't remember ever hearing before. His mother was crying.

His father walked up the hill and sat on the log next to Seth, and his mother sat crumpled on the running board of the truck, sobbing silently, her small body shaking so hard that the truck bounced on its shoddy old springs.

A deep, deep sadness washed over Seth. He really didn't care at all about the awful old house, but it was clear that his mother had experienced a greater loss. She looked so tired, so defeated.

Seth had never seen his mother look like this.

He knew that he shouldn't try to comfort her.

"Best just to let her be," his father said.

As much as Seth hated his mother's stubborn, ornery strength, he was sure he preferred that to this. His mother was always strong, no matter what.

He remembered walking home from school with a neighbor a few years back. Roland, his walking chum, was a year or two older and was full of wisdom that Seth was eager to absorb.

One day Roland pulled a box of matches from his pocket. He showed Seth how to throw the match just right, sort of like you'd throw a spear; and if you managed to hit it the right way on something hard, like a rock, the match would burst into flame. It was hard to do, but really fun.

Roland and Seth practiced throwing matches at rocks every day. They were getting very good at it. Then one day, a match bounced off into some dry grass, and the grass caught on fire. It all happened so fast. Seth and Roland stomped on the flames, but the wind was blowing and the flames spread quickly, and there were far too many flames for the boys to stomp out. The fire spread from farm to farm, burning acre after acre. Seth could still remember his parents coming home after hours of fighting the fire, their clothes and skin covered with soot. They were so tired they could barely propel their bodies forward. Dragging on the ground behind them were the burned, dirty, wet gunny sacks they had been using to beat back the flames. Seth would never forget the looks on their faces. Disappointment, anger, and disgust, all muted by their agonizing physical exhaustion. Seth never understood why he had been allowed to continue to live after doing something so very, very bad when so many other relatively minor infractions had brought him such beatings and punishment. He was, however, wise enough not to bring it up in order to find out. He had decided it was just as well to leave this as one of the great mysteries of the Universe.

As Seth thought back on that blackest of days, he actually wished his mother could be angry or exhausted now, instead of this. He had learned to cope with her anger, even when it was directed at him. But he had never seen her so broken.

"Where's Samuel?" Seth heard his mother's voice.

Seth was so happy his mother had spoken he had to stop and think where his little brother was.

"He got off the bus at Mrs. Whitaker's place. This is the day he mows her lawn. She said she'd bring him home when he's done if it's raining. Want me to go get him?"

"No, he'll be along. Get that big brush and see what you can do about sweeping out the feed room in the barn. Let's get a blanket up over the door.

And see if any of those old lanterns still work! I'll get the bucket and milk the goat. Gotta be careful with the milk," Seth heard his mother mutter. "That's all there'll be for supper."

Seth was always amazed at how well his mother dealt with crises. She was like an old drill sergeant, spouting commands and bringing order to things. And, for now, Seth really didn't mind that at all. The circumstances somehow seemed to create a new feeling of clarity; and Seth jumped into action, feeling alive and stimulated. He watched his mother corner the goat and begin to milk her. *Mother's something else,* Seth thought.

Rebuilding the house wasn't a possibility. It would require far more resources than the Morris family had, and besides, this wasn't their land anyway. The landlord had no insurance on the old shack and was absolutely not willing to rebuild it, so Seth's parents had decided, once again, that the family would move on.

CHAPTER 3

Who Is Solomon?

It was a warm and sunny afternoon in Sara's mountain town. In fact, Sara had decided earlier that this was the prettiest day so far this year. And to celebrate this extra-pretty day, she had decided to go to her favorite place in the whole town, her leaning perch. She called it *her* leaning perch because no one else in town even seemed to notice that it existed. Sara couldn't come to this spot without remembering how it came to be. How the metal railing atop the Main Street Bridge had been bent way out over the river when a local farmer had lost control of his truck while trying to avoid running over Harvey, a friendly and always roving dog, who weaved his way in and out of traffic every day, always expecting everyone to stop or swerve to make way for him. And, so far, it had always worked out that way. Sara was relieved that no one had been hurt that day, not even Harvey, who many thought deserved to get run over. *I've heard of cats having nine lives,* Sara thought to herself as she remembered that day, *but not dogs.*

Sara lay there, lazily watching the river flow by beneath her. She breathed deeply and enjoyed the wonderful smell of this delicious river. She couldn't remember ever feeling better. "I *love* my life!" Sara said right out loud, feeling a fresh exuberance and an eagerness for more.

"Well, better get going," Sara said to herself, climbing back out of her perch and gathering up her book bag and jacket that she had piled in a heap on the bridge. She was still standing on the bridge when the Morris family's rattling, sagging, overloaded truck drove across it. It wasn't the loud clanging of an out-of-tune engine, the crates of chickens tied to the roof, or the old goat teetering in the back of the truck that caught Sara's eye, but the intense, interested gaze of a boy riding in the back. His eyes locked with Sara's, and for a moment, they each felt as if they had met an old friend. Then the truck sputtered on down the road. Sara threw her bag over her shoulder and ran down the road to the intersection, looking to see where the truck pulled in. *It looks like it pulled into the old Thacker place,* she thought. *Hmm.*

Sara picked up her pace as she walked toward the Thacker house. She was intensely curious about what she would find.

Sara had heard that old Grandmother Thacker had passed away, but she hadn't given much thought to what would happen to her old house. Her husband had died even before Sara was born, and it seemed to her that Mrs. Thacker had been waving *Hello!* for Sara's whole life. Sara never knew her children, for they were all grown up and gone before she was old enough to walk around town by herself. Over the years, Sara had come to know the life patterns of this independent old woman, and it felt empty now that she was gone.

Sara had heard someone in the drugstore talking about Grandmother Thacker. (Everyone in town called her that.) "Her damn kids didn't even bother to come to her funeral," she heard Pete, the druggist, complain. "Bet they'll be around fast enough to collect any money she's left behind, though. You just wait and see."

As Sara walked, she felt worse and worse. And she knew why, too. "Solomon, I don't want anybody moving into Grandmother Thacker's house," she complained. "Solomon, can you hear me?"

"Who's Solomon? Who are you talking to?" Sara heard a boy's voice from behind her.

She wheeled around, startled that she had been overheard. She was certain that her face was turning bright red. *Where in the world did he come from?* she thought, embarrassed out of her mind. Sara just couldn't believe that this had happened.

She'd been caught, for the first time ever, talking to Solomon.

Sara was not *about* to answer his question. She had never told anyone about Solomon, and she certainly wasn't about to tell a total stranger this most important secret.

It was a pretty amazing story. She didn't know how she would ever get anyone to believe that she had met an owl last year on Thacker's Trail, the owl could actually talk, and that he called himself Solomon. And that even after her little brother, Jason, and his friend Billy had shot and killed Solomon, she was still able to have conversations with him. Sara knew no one would believe that she could hear Solomon's voice in her head.

There were times when Sara longed for someone to share this extraordinary experience with, but it felt too risky. If they misunderstood, they could ruin things. And Sara liked things the way they were with Solomon. She liked having this special friend all to herself—a wise and wonderful friend who had answers to anything that she could ask—a teacher who always seemed to appear just at the right time to help bring clarity to something that Sara was trying to understand.

"Don't be embarrassed. I talk to myself all the time, too." Seth said. "They say there's no need to worry unless you start answering yourself."

"Yeah, I guess," Sara stammered, still flushed

20

and embarrassed and looking mostly down. She took a deep breath and looked up. And there were those eyes again, familiar-seeming eyes like those of an old friend.

"I'm Seth. I guess we're going to live here, I mean, over *there*," he said, pointing in the direction of the old Thacker place.

"I'm Sara. I live past the river and down the road a ways." Sara's voice quivered as she spoke. This had really set her off balance.

"My dad sent me over to see if the creek water is clear, and to check out how far it is. I'd better get back."

Sara was relieved. All she wanted to do was run away, as far away as possible, from this strange new boy who hadn't even been in town for a whole hour and had already managed to intrude into the most important secret of her entire life.

CHAPTER 4

All Is Well

"Sara!" Seth called out to her.

Sara continued to move forward, turning to walk backward to see who it was. "Hey, how's it going?" she asked tentatively.

She stopped and waited for Seth to catch up to her, shifting her book bag to the other shoulder. She felt a strange mix of emotions. Part of her was sincerely drawn to Seth, while she didn't understand why; she had only just met him and really knew nothing about him. Another part of her wished that he would just go away—away from Grandmother Thacker's house, away from Thacker's Trail, and away from knowing anything about Solomon.

Seth ran to catch up with her, and as he reached her, he took off his jacket and tossed it over his shoulder. Sara felt tense, bracing herself for the inevitable next question, *Who's Solomon?*

"I'll carry that for you if you like," Seth said politely.

Sara stammered for a minute. She had been so sure he was going to ask about Solomon that she wasn't sure what he actually had said.

"What?"

"I was offering to carry your bag."

"Oh no, that's okay. I've got it." Sara took a deep breath and relaxed a little.

"Have you lived here long?"

"Yeah, all my life."

"All of your life? Really? That's amazing!"

Sara wasn't sure if it was good amazing or bad amazing.

"Why are you so surprised?" Sara asked. "Lots of people who live here have always lived here."

Seth was quiet. He was thinking about how many places his family had lived in his short life. He could barely imagine what it would be like to live in the same place your whole life. He longed for such stability. He'd never lived in one place even for one whole school term. He couldn't imagine being in a classroom with the same kids year after year after year. "Must be nice to have so many friends," Seth said.

"Well, they're not really my *friends*," Sara sighed. "Just because I know their names doesn't make them my friends. Where are *you* from?"

Seth laughed and scoffed at the same time.

"From?" Seth chided. "I'm from nowhere."

"Come on," Sara teased, "you have to be from *someplace*. Where did you live before you came here?"

"Arkansas. But we didn't live there very long. We never live anywhere very long."

"Must be fun," Sara said, thinking about how completely she had already explored her little mountain town. "I'd love to live in lots of different places. This place is so small, and there's so much out there to see."

Seth liked it that Sara seemed interested in his unstable life. Sara felt easier, too, finding that Seth wasn't pushing about Solomon.

They stopped in the middle of the intersection. This was the corner where Seth turned off to his house while Sara continued on down another block to hers. "I'd like to hear about some of the places you've lived."

"Yeah," Seth said, hesitantly. He really didn't want to tell Sara about any of that. He hadn't liked much of it. "Maybe you can show me around *here*. I'm sure there are some neat things to see."

"Sure," Sara replied, even though she was certain that this little town had very little to show Seth. He'd lived in so many different places. *Yeah, let's go off for an hour and I'll show you every place I know,* Sara thought sarcastically.

"See ya," Seth said, as he turned down his street.

"Yeah," Sara said.

Hello, Sara. Sara heard Solomon's voice in her head.

She quickly looked back at Seth. She had become so accustomed to hearing Solomon's voice that for a brief instant she thought maybe Seth had heard it, too.

At that moment, Seth was looking back at Sara. Sara waved an embarrassed half wave; so did Seth.

"Oh no, not again," Sara said under her breath. How did Seth keep getting into the middle of her conversations with Solomon? Sara didn't really believe that Seth had heard Solomon's voice, for no one else could *hear* his voice, but the whole set of circumstances and the timing of Solomon's chiming in had rattled her.

Sara wanted to make sure that Seth had gone on his way, so she waited until he turned the corner and was out of sight.

"Hi, Solomon."

I see you have met Seth.

"You know Seth?" Sara blurted, and then she smiled as she remembered that Solomon knows about everything.

Oh yes, Sara, I have been aware of Seth for quite some time now. I was pleased about the two of you meeting even before the two of you actually met.

"You *knew* that we would meet?"

*Seth's life experiences have produced many intensely
focused questions. I could feel him making his way into
<u>my</u> experience, and so, of course, it is logical that he
would also make his way into <u>your</u> experience, Sara. We
are all birds of a feather, you know.*

"Really, Solomon, Seth is like you and like
me?"

*He is, indeed, Sara. An intense seeker, a born up-
lifter—and a true teacher.*

Sara felt a pang of discomfort. She had come to
adore her relationship with Solomon. She wasn't
so sure she wanted to share that with this strange
new boy.

*All is well, Sara. All is extremely well. We will all
have a wonderful time together.*

"Well, if you say so, Solomon."

Sara could see her younger brother, Jason, running to catch up with her, but she'd had enough
of people listening in on her conversations with
Solomon.

"Thanks, Solomon, I'll catch you later."

Solomon smiled. Sara was growing up so
quickly.

CHAPTER 5

Seth Has Found Thacker's Trail

"Hey, Sara, what's up?" Sara looked up from her book and smiled as Seth slid into the chair next to her in the school's upstairs, hardly ever used, library. The librarian looked up with a stern glare, wanting to hush these two who were openly talking in the library. "Oh, nothing much," Sara whispered.

Not wanting Seth to get involved in her journal, she quickly closed her book. One of the things Sara loved most about school was putting together a journal on some special subject for one of her classes. Although she wasn't really a very good artist, she loved clipping associated articles, pictures, or anything that fit into the subject, and arranging them neatly on pages for her class. Her journals were often regarded as excellent by her teachers, and were nearly always equally scorned by her classmates. She knew that she usually went overboard, but the approval of the teachers some-how outweighed the disapproval of her classmates; and so, mostly happily, Sara journaled on.

This journal was about leaves. Sara had gathered hundreds of leaves from trees and bushes and ditch banks and flower gardens, and was now doing her best to identify them. She had books about leaves spread out all over the table in front of her but had really only identified a fraction of them. She was surprised at how little she really knew about the things that were around her, and had been around her all of her life. There is so much to know.

"You like leaves?" Seth asked, seeing the books opened in front of Sara.

"Yeah, I guess," Sara answered, pretending boredom. "I'm really just trying to figure out what *kinds* of leaves I've gathered. It's for a class. I'm not very good at it."

"I know about leaves," Seth offered. "Or at least I know about the leaves where I *used* to live. They're different here, but some are the same. I'll go with you if you want and show you the leaves I know. If you want, I mean."

Sara didn't really like the idea of anyone get-ting involved in one of her projects. That hadn't worked out very well for her in the past. Sara often described herself as "all or nothing," meaning she often went very much overboard when she got involved in a project, or if the project didn't interest her, she didn't touch it at all. And rarely did anyone else share her outrageous enthusiasm—or absolute lack of enthusiasm—for a subject. And nearly always, feelings would get hurt.

"Oh, I don't know," Sara hesitated. "I'm probably better off doing this by myself."

"Okay, I understand," Seth said, "but if you change your mind, let me know. It sure is a lot easier to find something in a book if you have an idea of what it's called, and I know lots of names of trees and bushes and stuff. My Grandpa knows all of them. He makes medicine with them and eats them. He says that anything you would ever need grows right out in the open where anyone can find them, but almost no one knows they're even there."

Seth had made a good point. Sara had spent the better part of her lunch hour looking through book after book before she found a picture of the big red leaf she had pressed in her journal. Seth could save her lots of time, and he seemed nice enough, not too pushy or anything.

"Well, okay, then. You want to go after school today?"

"Okay," Seth said. "I'll meet you by the flagpole. I found a cool place last weekend, not too far from here, over by the creek, not far from the tree crossing. It's a neat trail with lots of big old trees and bushes. We'll go there."

Mrs. Horton stood up with a big scowl on her face. It was bad enough that Seth and Sara had been talking out loud, but now Seth was calling clear across the room.

The door banged closed, and Sara's body jumped as she realized he was talking about Thacker's Trail. *Seth has found Thacker's Trail!*

CHAPTER 6

Coming Back to Life?

Sara waited by the flagpole. *I can't believe I agreed to do this,* she grumbled under her breath. *I mean, Thacker's Trail is my secret place. . . . I guess I knew he'd find it sooner or later. I just thought it would be later.*

She looked at her watch and said to herself, "Where is he?" Then she noticed a folded piece of paper sticking out of the base of the flagpole with "Sara" written on it in very small print. She opened the note and read it: *Sara, meet me at our corner. I have something neat to show you. It's a leaf-covered jungle trail. See ya!*

Sara felt such an odd mix of emotions. She had already really come to like Seth. And she liked the idea that someone who had lived in so many places would find something that interested him in this little mountain town that Sara had known all of her life. But the idea of him discovering her special secret place so soon didn't feel good to Sara.

As Sara approached the corner where Seth always turned off to go to his house, she saw a rock right in the middle of the intersection with another piece of paper fluttering in the wind beneath it. "What in the world?" Sara laughed. "This is a very odd boy."

The note said: *Turn right, cross over the bridge, go past my house, and then immediately left. There's a trail, hard to see, but it's there. Follow it. I'll meet you.*

Well, there was no doubt now—Seth had found Thacker's Trail.

"Well, of course he's found it. How could he not? He practically lives right on it," Sara grumbled, feeling resentful that the inevitable had happened.

Sara wadded the note and put it in her pocket. "Like I need directions to find *my* trail," she said out loud. She crossed the bridge and passed Seth's house and turned down her beloved, and oh-so-familiar, Thacker's Trail.

As she walked, the memories of this trail began moving through her mind so clearly it was as if she were watching a movie. She remembered her reluctant trek there at the insistence of her little brother, Jason, who had seemed driven in a way Sara had never seen before, and how he insisted that there was a giant owl named Solomon hiding somewhere in the woods. She remembered them looking in vain, and how disappointed she had felt that no owl was found, but she would never have admitted her disappointment to her pesky little brother.

As Sara walked down the long, dark path, she began to relax back into the quiet and peace of this trail. Then she broke into a big smile as she rounded the corner and saw the fence post where Solomon had been sitting that day. Her eyes filled with tears as she remembered this big, sweet, loving, and oh-so-very-wise owl just sitting there waiting for her.

It's strange, Sara thought. *Solomon is still very much a part of my life. I mean, we still visit nearly every single day. But I do miss seeing his beautiful body and looking into his wonderful eyes.*

Sara felt a bit ashamed that she still missed Solomon in his physical form. She understood what Solomon meant when he had explained that "there is no death," and she certainly knew that their relationship was continuing. And, on most days, Sara never even thought about the old Solomon, and she absolutely enjoyed her *now* Solomon. But being here, where they had first met, only a few feet from where Jason and Billy had shot him, was putting Sara off her usual balance, and she was missing her old physical, feathered friend.

Out of the corner of her eye she noticed something moving in the leaves, and her heart jumped right into her throat when she realized that this movement was happening on the very spot where Solomon had died. For a moment Sara thought, *Maybe he has decided to come back to life.*

What in the world is that!? Sara strained her eyes trying to make out whatever was moving beneath the leaves in the shadows of the thicket.

As Sara got closer, she gasped and jumped back. There, lying in the leaves on the very spot where Solomon had died, was Seth. He was half covered in leaves and his eyes were closed, and his tongue was hanging out of the side of his mouth.

Sara couldn't speak. She just stood there, paralyzed. "Ss. . . sss . . . Seth," she stuttered, "are you all right?"

She knew he *couldn't* be all right. He looked *awful.* Sara stood and stared; she bit her lip so hard it began to bleed, and tears flowed down her cheeks.

"Geez, Sara, don't take it so hard. I was only kidding!" Seth quipped as he jumped to his feet, brushing the leaves out of his hair.

"I hate you!" Sara blurted, turning and running away from Seth and from the thicket. "How could you do that to me?" she cried, running away as fast as she could.

Seth was stunned. He had no idea that Sara would react this way. He didn't know why he had felt compelled to lie on the ground, half covering his body with leaves, pretending death or at least severe injury. The idea just seemed to come out of nowhere. A very *bad* idea, he now realized.

"Sara, wait, what's the matter?" Seth called. "Hey, can't you take a joke? Hey, don't you want to look for leaves?"

Sara didn't answer.

CHAPTER 7

A Born Uplifter

It had felt like a very long day at school.
Sara knew that Seth was running to catch up with her, but she had decided not to stop and wait for him. She was still mad at him for his awful prank yesterday, and she wasn't going to give in to him so easily. In fact, she had pretty much decided never to talk to him again.

Seth didn't understand why what seemed to him like an innocent and potentially very funny prank had affected Sara so negatively. He had no way of knowing that the spot he had chosen was the exact place on which Sara's beloved Solomon had actually died.

Seth caught up with Sara. "Hey," Seth said softly.

Sara didn't answer.

They walked, neither speaking. Seth thought of many things he might say, but when he practiced them in his mind they all seemed wrong.

Jason, Sara's little brother, and his friend Billy raced by on their bicycles. "Sara's got a boyfriend, Sara's got a boyfriend," they chided in unison as they passed by.

"Shut up!" Sara yelled back.

A cat scurried across the sidewalk right in front of Sara and Seth. The cat startled Seth, and he jumped a funny little jump in the air. Sara managed to contain her laughter, but she couldn't stop her grin altogether. It broke the icy tension.

"That cat reminds me of one we used to have," Seth said.

Sara watched the cat run off into the bushes. She had tried to catch that very cat many times, but never could. He was wild and mangy and fast.

"Oh yeah?" Sara said, trying hard to stay mad at Seth.

"We called our cat Tripod," Seth said, hoping to get some sort of response from Sara.

It worked.

"Tripod?" Sara questioned and laughed at the same time. "What a weird name."

"Well," Seth said, looking down with a very sad face, "he only had three legs."

Sara blurted out her laugh. It wasn't nice to laugh about a poor crippled cat, but the shock of a three-legged cat in combination with his three-legged name was too much for Sara to contain.

Seth was very pleased that Sara was talking to him again.

"What happened to Tripod's leg?" Sara asked.

"We never found out. Probably got caught in a trap or something. Maybe a snake."

Sara winced.

"Yeah, we had a two-legged cat once, too," Seth said with great seriousness. "We called him Roo, you know, short for kangaroo."

Sara laughed, imagining a cat springing around on its back legs, but she was suspicious that Seth was making *this* one up. What were the odds of having a three-legged cat *and* a two-legged cat?

"Geez, your family sure was hard on cats!"

"Yeah," Seth said, very seriously. "We once had a one-legged cat, too."

"Yeah, right," Sara quipped. Now she was sure Seth was making it all up. "What did you call *that* cat? Pogo stick?"

"Nope, we called him Cyclops. He only had one eye, too."

Sara burst out laughing. It felt so much better to be entertained by Seth than to be mad at him.

They came to the corner where Seth turned off to his house. Seth grinned, feeling glad that he had managed to make Sara laugh and play with him again. And Sara continued on down the country road toward her house. She laughed and laughed and laughed. She wasn't sure if Seth had a strange knack for turning tragedy into comedy, or if he was just the funniest person she'd ever met. But in any case, Sara could not remember ever having laughed so hard. *He probably never even had a cat.* Sara grinned.

"Hey, Sara, was that your little brother on the bicycle?" Seth yelled back at her.

"Yeah, that's him," Sara called back. "I knew you'd meet him sooner or later. I just hoped it would be later. *Much* later."

"Hey, Seth," Sara called out loudly, not sure if Seth was too far away to hear her.

Seth turned around, smiling, and stopped.

"I thought cats are supposed to have nine lives."

"Oh, we don't kill 'em, we just maim 'em," Seth called back. "And I think it's more like 14, but I lost count on some of them."

Sara laughed again.

"I think that goes for people, too!" Seth yelled.

Sara continued on down the road. She didn't know what to make of Seth. His life seemed mysterious, and in some ways tragic, but he was very interesting. And he was funny. Was he making it up to be funny, or was he making it funny to keep it from being so tragic? And what was this business about having 14 lives? Was he kidding about that, too?

We are all birds of a feather, you know. Sara remembered Solomon's words: *Seth is an intense seeker, a born uplifter—and a true teacher.*

Sara smiled. "This is going to be very interesting," she said out loud.

CHAPTER 8

Solomon Peeks In

Sara sat on her front porch enjoying being the only one home. Her parents were still at work, and her little brother nearly always found something to do after school. She leaned against the post and thought about Solomon.

"Hi, Solomon, have you missed me?"

No, Sara, not at all. Sara heard Solomon's voice come right back to her.

Sara laughed. She and Solomon had exchanged those very words many times. The first time Solomon had responded in that way, Sara felt surprised and even hurt. "What do you mean you haven't missed me at all?" she had asked.

Solomon explained, then, that he was always aware of Sara. Even though she might not be thinking of him or talking with him, he was always fully aware of her. Therefore, there would be no reason to miss her because she was never away from his awareness. Sara liked that.

At first it felt odd for someone to be aware of her at all times. She didn't much like the idea that no matter where she was or what she was doing, Solomon was peeking in. But in time, once Sara got to know Solomon better, she found she didn't mind him peeking into her life at all, because Solomon always seemed pleased with what he saw. He never scolded Sara for inappropriate behavior; he never seemed displeased with something she had done. Instead, Solomon continued to offer his unconditional love and guided Sara only when she asked for guidance.

"How have you been?" Sara chirped, knowing full well what Solomon's response would be, but wanting to hear it anyway just because it always felt so good.

I am splendid, Sara, and I see that you are as well.

"Yep," Sara answered happily. She could never remember being happier.

I have noticed that you and your new friend, Seth, are having a marvelous time together. That is very good.

"We are, Solomon. I've never had so much fun with anyone. It's weird. He's not like anyone I've ever known. He's serious but funny; he's very smart but silly and playful; and he has a really hard life at home, but he's light and easy when he's with me. I can't figure him out."

He is one of those rare humans who has learned to live in the moment. Rather than carrying forward the feeling from something that has happened before, he is allowing himself to respond to the clarity of your moment together. He likes being with you, too, Sara.

"Did he tell you that?" Then Sara laughed, realizing as soon as she spoke that Solomon didn't have to have a conversation with someone to know what they thought. He always knew what people were thinking and feeling.

Seth wants more than anything to feel good, and so, being with you feels just right to him. You bring out the best in him, Sara.

"Well, I want to. But I'm not *trying* to do that, Solomon. It just happens. I think he brings out the best in me."

Well, I'm very pleased that you two are having such a wonderful time together. It is always nice to meet another who wants to feel good, too. When two people get together and they both hold the same desire of feeling good, great things always come from that.

You are both uplifters, Sara, and nothing pleases an uplifter more than helping another feel better. That's what uplifting is.

You will have a wonderful time together, Sara. I am certain of that.

43

CHAPTER 9

Geronimooooo . . . Splat!

The last bell had rung nearly 15 minutes ago, and Sara waited by the flagpole in front of the school building. She watched the big doors open and bang shut as student after student left the building. She had promised to wait for Seth; he said he had something to show her that he was sure she'd really like. She looked at her watch, wondering if she'd somehow misunderstood their meeting plans, and then, once more, the big doors opened and there was Seth. At last!

"Sorry, Sara. I made the mistake of saying hello to Miss Ralph, and she asked me if I could help her load her car. I said I would, but I had no idea her car was parked a mile away, and I had no idea she had 47 loads of stuff. I knew as soon as I said hello that I'd made a big mistake, but I couldn't take it back."

Sara laughed. She'd made plenty of those trips to Miss Ralph's car herself. Miss Ralph was the school's art director, and it seemed to Sara that she hauled half of her possessions back and forth between her home and school every day.

"I never walk past her room," Sara said. "I used to, but now I go way around." She laughed again.

"I thought the hallway was strangely empty," Seth said. "I guess everyone except me knew she was lurking there looking for a helper."

Sara really didn't mind helping Miss Ralph. She had never taken one of her classes, but she was actually rather impressed that this pretty new teacher was willing to work so hard to offer a good art program.

"I don't mind helping her," Seth said. "She sure works hard."

Sara smiled. It was as if he were reading her mind.

"I just didn't know it would take so long, and I didn't like keeping you waiting. Ready?"

"Yeah," Sara said. "What's up?"

"It's a surprise."

"Tell me!" Sara blurted.

Seth laughed. "No, you have to *see* it. It's not far from Thacker's Trail."

Sara felt a pang of discomfort again. Nobody else, as far as Sara knew, spent any time on or around Thacker's Trail. And that suited Sara just fine; she liked having it all to herself.

They walked down the rutty road and then ducked off the road onto Thacker's Trail.

"You know," Seth said, "we should find some other way in here. We don't want this path getting too obvious."

Sara smiled. *He does read my mind,* she thought.

Sara followed Seth single file down the narrow path. He held the branches back so they wouldn't slap back into her face, and occasionally waved his hands up over his head to knock a spider web out of the way.

"Hey, this is great!" Sara said.

"What?"

"Following you. That way the cobwebs end up in *your* hair, not mine."

Seth laughed, pulling a streamer of spider web from his face. "You wanna lead?" he teased.

"No, that's okay. You're doing fine."

They came to the first of several forks in the trail, and Seth led off toward the river. Sara followed briskly to keep up.

The trail became almost nonexistent, and Seth and Sara stepped high in the very deep, dry grass. And just as Sara was about to stop to remove the thistle burrs from her socks, they broke out into the opening right at the edge of the river.

"Oh, this is a *great* spot," Sara said. "I'd forgotten how pretty the river is right here. I haven't been here in a long time."

"Okay, here it is!" Seth said, proudly.

"Here, what is?" Sara asked, looking around to see what was different.

"Back here," Seth said, guiding Sara around to the back of the tree. Sara looked up at the giant cottonwood tree. "Whoa!" Sara exclaimed. "You did this?"

"Yeah, ya like it?" Seth asked.

"This is amazing!" Sara could hardly believe what she was seeing. Seth had nailed boards about every ten inches from the base of the tree all the way up into the tree limbs. They were long enough so that they extended out beyond the width of the tree trunk. They not only made perfect foot rails, but while you were standing on those below, you could use the ones above for hand-holds. "This is the very best tree ladder I've ever seen."

"I sanded them real good so you won't get slivers in your hands," Seth said proudly.

"This is great! Let's go up!"

"I'll go first," Seth said.

Seth stepped up onto the first board and reached up to another one to pull himself up. He climbed easily up, up, up.

Sara giggled with delight. She loved climbing trees and could hardly believe that Seth had made it so amazingly easy to get way up inside of this great old tree.

They climbed high into the tree. "I love this,"

Sara said. "The whole world looks different from up here, doesn't it?"

Seth agreed as he shimmied out onto a branch way out over the river. Sara noticed how sure of himself he seemed to be even though the river was far below. Sara couldn't see what he was doing because whatever it was, it was hidden by his body. And then she saw a long, heavy rope drop down from the branch, almost down to the water.

"I don't believe it!" Sara shouted, in glee.

"Wanna try it?" Seth could hardly contain himself.

"You bet!"

"How's your balance?" Seth asked.

"Pretty good, I guess. Why?"

"Because now we have to get over *there.*"

Sara looked to where Seth was pointing. "A tree house! Seth, you've made a tree house!"

"That is our launching pad," Seth said, carefully crawling on this hands and knees out onto a large limb. He crawled a long way out and then stood up.

Sara kneeled down and crawled carefully out to the tree house. *I hope it's big enough for two of us,* she thought tentatively. But when she arrived and stood up, she was pleasantly surprised at how big it was. Seth had even built a back railing for safety and support and two little benches to sit on.

Sara watched with pleasure as Seth demonstrated how all of this worked. Wrapped around a nail was a thin twine. He unwrapped it from the nail and then began winding it around a stick that was stuck in a crack in the bark.

"You've thought of everything!" Sara said in delight.

Seth had tied the twine to the bottom of the big heavy rope that was dangling down to the water below. As he continued to wrap the twine around his stick, the twine pulled the big rope right up into the tree, right to where Sara and Seth were standing. At the bottom of the heavy, long rope, Seth had tied a loop, and Sara watched as he sat on one of the benches and put his foot in the loop. There were three knots tied in the rope above the loop. Seth took hold of the top knot and said, "Okay, wish me luck."

"Be careful . . ." Sara began, but before she could finish her sentence, Seth jumped off the platform. He swung way out over the river, yelling, "Geronimoooooooo!" as he flew. It took Sara's breath away just to watch. He swung back and forth, traveling a little less distance with each pass.

"Now, here's the tricky part," Seth called. "You have to jump off before the rope stops swinging, or else you have to wade out of the river."

Sara watched Seth as he struggled to free his foot from the loop, locking his knees around one of the lower knots in the rope. And as he swung out close to the riverbank, he leaped from the rope and tumbled into a pile of leaves. "Ouch!" Sara heard Seth's muffled voice. "This part needs work."

Sara laughed, delighted at all that she'd seen.

"Okay, it's my turn," Sara said excitedly, as Seth quickly climbed back up the tree.

"I don't know, Sara. The landing is a bit rough. Maybe you should wait until I figure—"

"Nope, I'm going. If you can do it, I can do it!" There was no possible way that Sara wasn't going to swing out over the river.

Sara waited, excited, as she watched Seth climbing up into the tree. *He's such a clever boy,* she thought, as she realized that Seth was carrying the end of the twine back up the tree with him so that he could again pull the big, heavy swinging rope back up to the launching pad.

Sara sat on the bench and Seth held the heavy rope so Sara could put her foot in the loop. "I made *this* knot for you, Sara," Seth said, pointing out the second knot that seemed just right for Sara's body size.

"Okay, I'm going to go!" Sara said, still standing on the platform. "Okay, here I go . . . I'm ready now. . . I'm going now. . . I'll be right back . . . Here I go . . . I'm outta here!" Sara giggled. She wanted to go so much she could hardly stand it, but the idea of jumping out of the tree made her stomach tingle with excitement—and she just couldn't quite push off.

Seth watched and smiled, enjoying Sara's excitement. He was not about to make this decision for her. "There's no hurry, Sara. This rope will be here tomorrow and the day after and the day after that . . ."

But Sara didn't hear what Seth was saying, because in the middle of giving her an excuse *not* to jump, she leaped right off the platform and flew through the air.

"Geronimooooooo!" she squealed as she flew out over the river.

"All right!" Seth called, so pleased that Sara had taken the first big plunge, and remembering his own immense pleasure in his first scary swing across a river. He could hear Sara laughing and squealing as she flew back and forth across the river, and then he watched her as she pulled her foot out of the loop.

Thatta girl! he said under his breath, pleased that she had learned so quickly how to dismount. But Sara's arms weren't as strong as Seth's, and once her foot was out of the loop she had a hard time holding onto the swinging rope. She managed to hold on until her body was closer to the river's edge, but then she let go, flying through the air into the muddy river bank. Splat! Water splashed. Mud flew in the air. And Sara laughed. She stood up, soaking wet from head to toe and covered in mud, laughing and laughing and laughing.

Seth watched in horror, and then he began to laugh in relief. *What a good sport this girl is!* He felt responsible for her ride and for her safety, so he was truly relieved that this was turning out so well.

"Seth, this is great! I can't wait to do this again. You gotta show me how to get *off* of this ride, though."

"It's mostly about timing your jump. I got wet the first time I jumped off, too."

"You did not." Sara knew from watching Seth that he'd known exactly what he was doing. But she liked the idea that he was trying to make her feel more adequate by appearing not quite so adequate himself.

"That's okay. I'm glad you're good at this. I'll get good at it, too. We'll practice every day. I love this, Seth! Thank you for making this for us."

Seth didn't know what to make of Sara. She was so great to be with. She was eager and willing to do just about anything. She was such a good sport; she laughed easily, and it didn't bother her that someone else was better at something than she was. Seth had never known anyone like Sara.

"I'd better get home. I'm a mess," Sara said, dragging herself out of the water and tugging at her wet, muddy clothing. "I'll see ya tomorrow."

"Tomorrow's Saturday," Seth reminded Sara,

knowing that his parents wouldn't permit his taking time away from the busy weekend chores to play. He had built this tree house, mostly by moonlight, over a period of many weeks. His parents would never allow this kind of frivolous behavior. "We can swing again on Monday."

"Oh," Sara said, disappointed. She didn't know how she could possibly wait until Monday to have more of this fun. "Okay," Sara said, "but I think I'm going to come here tomorrow by myself and practice my dismount. By Monday, when I see you, I'll have it down."

Seth did not like that idea one bit. What if Sara let go at the wrong time and broke her leg or hit her head or worse. "No, Sara, you could drown," Seth blurted, feeling a little embarrassed as the words left his mouth.

Sara paused and looked at Seth, hearing the intensity of his offering; he had projected his concern in a very loud, clear way.

"No, Seth," Sara said softly. "I can never drown."

Seth saw an intensity in Sara that he hadn't seen before. *How can she possibly be so certain that she won't drown?*

"But I'll wait until Monday. Since you went to all this trouble of making this great place for us, the least I could do is wait for you to share it with me."

Seth was relieved.

"I'll see ya Monday," Sara said. "I'll wait by the first fork in the trail."

Seth smiled. Sara had read his mind. He didn't want their rendezvous to be so obvious that others wondered where they were going. Both Seth and Sara liked the idea of keeping this great hideaway all to themselves.

CHAPTER 10

Snakes Won't Bother You

Sara was waiting for Seth at the first fork in the trail. She mentally complimented herself for wearing brown and tan clothing that blended well into her surroundings. She laughed at herself as she crouched down close to the ground, secretly waiting for her partner to rendezvous. She saw an occasional glitter of light through the bushes as passing cars drove down the road reflecting sunlight in her direction. She liked the idea that she could see them but they were unaware of her. "I hope Miss Ralph didn't nab him again," Sara muttered.

Seth blasted through the trees, nearly running Sara over. They both let out a startled scream, and then laughed. "Geez, Sara, I didn't think you were in here."

"Pretty good, huh?" Sara grinned, feeling rather proud of her camouflage.

"Yeah, you blend right in. If you'd a been a snake, you woulda had me for sure."

"Nah, snakes won't bother you," Sara said assuredly.

"You're not afraid of *snakes?*" Seth was surprised. He thought everybody was afraid of snakes. Especially girls.

"No, I used to be, but I'm not anymore. Let's get going. I wanna swing from the trees."

Seth couldn't help but notice that Sara had the same intense sureness about not being afraid of snakes that she'd had about knowing that she wouldn't drown.

"Hey, Sara, how come you were so sure that you could never drown?"

Sara nearly stumbled on the path. Seth's question had caught her by surprise. Here he was again, zeroing in on what was maybe the most important experience—as well as the biggest secret—of her life.

"Oh, it's a pretty long story," Sara said. "I'll tell you later."

Seth sensed that Sara had something that she wanted to tell him, and he wanted to hear it. "Well, if it's a long story, maybe you should break it into pieces. You know? Give me a little more every day."

Sara felt uncomfortable with Seth's prodding. She wasn't sure how he would feel about her if she explained the details of her experience with Solomon. But there was an intensity about Seth that was compelling.

And so, Sara began. "Well, I never really thought I'd drown, but my mother worried about it all the time. She warned me just about every day of my life to stay away from this river. I don't know why *she* is so afraid of the river. I don't know of anybody who has ever drowned in it. But she worries about everything, especially the river.

"So one day when I was all by myself, I was standing out in the middle of the crossing log, and the water was really high, you know? It was even washing up over the log a little, when this big old fuzzy dog just came out of nowhere and knocked me right into the river!"

"Wow, Sara! What did you do?"

"Well, there wasn't anything I *could* do. The water was really moving fast, and it just carried me away. But I wasn't scared or anything. At first, I thought, *Oh no, my mother is right. And, boy, is she going to be mad at me if I drown.* But then I just floated and noticed how beautiful it all was. And then I floated under a tree branch that was dangling down into the water, and I pulled myself out. And from then on, I knew that I would never drown."

"That's it? That's how you know you won't drown? Sara, sounds to me like you were pretty lucky that you floated under the tree limb. You *could've* drowned, you know?"

Sara watched Seth as he let his negative imagination run away with him, and then she smiled. "You sound like my mother."

Seth laughed. "I guess I do."

"Don't you ever *know* things? I mean, don't you ever just know something, and you know it so clearly that it doesn't matter what anyone else thinks about it? You know because you know. And just because they don't know it doesn't mean that *you* don't know it. You know what I mean?"

Seth was quiet as Sara spoke. He did know what she meant. He knew exactly what she meant. "You're right, Sara. I do know what you mean. And from now on, if you say you can't drown, I'll believe you."

Sara was relieved that Seth had accepted her partial explanation and that she didn't have to explain further.

"Good." Sara felt triumphant. She wanted to change the subject. "And snakes won't bother you either!"

Seth laughed. "Well, let's just slash one deadly fear at a time, Sara."

CHAPTER 11

Practice in Your Mind?

Sara and Seth rounded the last bend in the trail and came into the clearing where Seth's wonderful tree house and swinging rope seemed to be patiently waiting for their return.

"Okay, I'll go first," Sara said, as she climbed quickly up into the tree. She crawled out onto the big branch and positioned herself on the platform while Seth caught up with her. "Okay. I'm going to get this right. I've been practicing."

Seth was disappointed that Sara hadn't kept her word. "Sara, you said you'd wait for me."

"I *did* wait for you, Seth. I've been practicing in my mind. Over and over, I saw myself swinging out across the river, and then, just at the perfect moment, I would let go of the rope and land perfectly on the grass on the other side. I'm ready, Seth. Give me a big push."

"I don't think you need a push, Sara. Just fall

out of the tree. That'll be plenty."

Off Sara went. "Yahooooooo!" she shouted, as she flew through the air, her pretty brown hair blowing straight out behind her. She flew back and forth, back and forth, slowing a bit with each pass over the river. *She pulled her foot from the loop, and then, at the perfect moment, she let go of the rope and landed in the grass right on the spot she had practiced in her mind.* Her landing was so perfect she didn't even fall down, but instead she absorbed the shock of her jump with her knees. *"Yes!"* she shouted in glee.

Seth applauded from the tree house. He was impressed.

Seth swung from the tree and then let go of the rope and crashed into the leaves as he'd done before. "Not a smooth landing," he noted.

Sara smiled. "You need to practice in your mind. That's all. It doesn't take long. And it's almost as much fun as really jumping."

"Okay." Seth seemed distracted. "But for now, I think I'll practice with the tree and the river and the rope." And up the tree he went again.

His landing this time was even worse than the last two times. He was *not* pleased.

Sara laughed and then covered her face with her hand, pretending that she was coughing. She didn't want to hurt his feelings, and she didn't want to make him mad.

Again, Seth climbed the tree, and again his timing was off and he rolled into the leaves.

He climbed the tree again, and this time Sara climbed right up behind him.

"Seth," Sara said, as he put his foot in the loop getting ready to leap into the air again, "wait just a minute. Stop and close your eyes and imagine climbing up the tree again, really happy because you just made the perfect landing. Pretend that I'm smiling and clapping."

"And laughing and coughing," Seth teased.

"No, just smiling and clapping." Sara grinned. *Nothing gets by Seth,* she thought.

"Now, see yourself releasing the rope and jumping onto the bank. Like landing with a parachute and dropping softly to the ground."

Seth smiled as he imagined.

"Now, go," Sara said, softly touching Seth's back, giving him a light nudge. And off he went.

He swung way out over the river. And then at the perfect moment, he let go of the rope and landed perfectly on the grass and then jumped into the air, clicking his heels together. "Yes!" he shouted, at the very same time that Sara shouted, "Yes!"

"Man! Sara, that really works. How'd you learn to do that?"

"Oh, a little bird told me," Sara teased. "It's a really long story, Seth."

And before Seth could say anything, Sara laughed and continued, "I know, I know, I'll break it down into short chapters for you and give you a little bit of it every day. If you really want to know, Seth, I'll tell you the whole story, but you have to promise not to laugh—and you have to promise not to ever tell anyone."

"I promise," Seth said. He had never seen Sara so intense before. "I promise. Now tell me."

"Later," Sara said. "I have to practice this in my mind first."

Seth grinned.

"See ya," Sara said.

"Yeah. I'll see ya tomorrow."

CHAPTER 12

Weird in a Good Way

Sara sat in a comfortable fork high up in the swinging tree. She'd climbed up the ladder all the way to its end and then had climbed up still another ten feet or so to a nice wide fork in the tree, big enough for the two of them to sit. *This is an amazing tree,* Sara thought as she sat quietly waiting for Seth.

His last class of the day was a woodworking class. *I'll bet he's good at that class. He's probably helping the teacher clean up the whole shop,* Sara thought, looking at her watch. *He's so nice. People take advantage of him.*

Sara leaned back in the tree and tried to imagine explaining her amazing story to Seth. She felt strongly that he was really ready to hear the story, but she also felt a strong sense of risk. He had become a very good friend. In fact, he was just about the best friend Sara had ever had, and she sure didn't like the idea of frightening him away. She couldn't really be sure how he would react to her secret.

A gust of wind swept through the trees, moving the leaves and smaller branches, and a flutter of dust and leaves showered down from above.

You, too, are a teacher, Sara remembered Solomon's strong words to her. *And when the timing is right, you will know.*

I think the timing is right, Sara thought. *But how do I know for sure?*

When there is asking, the timing is right. Sara remembered Solomon's advice. *Well, Seth sure has been asking,* Sara thought. *I guess it is time.*

Sara heard a rustling on the trail below. Standing up and holding tightly to a big branch above her, she leaned out as far as she could to see who was coming. Seth came blasting in from the bushes and called a breathless, "Hi, sorry I took so long." He was so winded, Sara knew he had run all the way.

He climbed up the tree and stopped on the big branch that led out to the platform. "Should I come up to where you are, or do you want to come down?"

"Come up here. It's great. And there's plenty of room," Sara called back. She liked the greater feeling of privacy far up in the tree.

Seth climbed up and propped himself in a big

V across from Sara. "So," Seth started right in, "tell me."

"Okay. But remember, this is *our* secret."

"Sara, don't worry. You're the only one I ever talk to, anyway."

Sara took a big breath and tried to find a starting place. There was so much to tell that she really didn't know where to begin.

"Okay, Seth. Here's what happened. But I'm warning you. It's going to sound weird."

"Sara," Seth sounded impatient, "I won't think it's weird. What *is* it?"

"Well, one day I was walking home from school when my brother, Jason, came running up to me, more excited than I had ever seen him, blubbering that there was a giant owl over on Thacker's Trail and that I just had to go and see it. He was so intense it was scary. And he halfway dragged me over to the trail."

"I love owls," Seth chimed in, wanting to encourage Sara to go on.

"Well, anyway, the snow was really deep, and it was a very cold day. We looked for a long time but didn't see any owl. And I told Jason he was making the whole thing up and that I didn't care about any stupid bird, anyway. But the next day in school, I couldn't stop thinking about this owl. And I couldn't figure out why I was so interested; the whole thing just felt weird to me. Anyway, after school I went back to the thicket by myself to look for him again, but I still couldn't find him. It was getting dark and I was feeling pretty stupid, and then I tried to take a shortcut by walking on the ice across the river, but the ice gave way under my feet and I fell down—I thought I was going to fall through the ice and drown. And then I heard a voice coming from the tree. It said, *Have you forgotten that you cannot drown?* And then the voice said, *The ice will hold you. Crawl over here.*

"At first I felt so dumb because I should have known better than to get out on the ice like that, and then I was mad that whoever was talking to me wouldn't come out where I could see him and help me. And then it hit me. How did he know I couldn't drown? I had never told even one other soul about that. And then I saw him."

"Saw who?"

"I saw Solomon. This gigantic, beautiful, magical owl. He flew up out of the tree and circled around the pasture, nice and slow so I could see him really well, and then he flew away. And I *knew* I'd found Solomon."

"Now I see why you were so sure you won't drown. Geez, Sara, that *is* weird. But it's weird in a good way," he added quickly.

Sara sat, almost breathless. She gulped and took a big breath and looked at Seth. She wanted to tell him everything about Solomon. How they had met, and all that he'd taught her, and how Jason and Billy had shot and killed him, and how even though he had been killed, he was still able to talk to Sara.

"Did you ever see him again?" Seth asked.

"Yes, I saw him a whole bunch of times. But then . . ."

"Then, *what?*" Seth was so interested in this amazing story.

Sara just couldn't bring herself to go any further. "I'll tell you about it later."

Seth was disappointed. He knew Sara had much more to tell him. He could feel it. But he also knew this was a tender subject with Sara, and he didn't want to push her.

"Well, I told you that I'd tell you this a little bit at a time. So, I'll see you tomorrow?"

"Yeah. Tomorrow."

"Wanna swing once before we go?" Sara asked.

"I think I've had enough excitement for now," Seth teased.

"Yeah, me too," Sara said.

"See ya."

Chapter 13

Friends of a Feather

"It's almost like daylight," Sara muttered under her breath as she leaned against the porch railing, gazing into the night sky. She felt irritable but didn't know why.

The sky was overcast and the stadium lights from the high-school football field were blazing brightly. It seemed to Sara on a night like this that those lights lit up the whole town.

"What a waste of electricity," Sara muttered, going into the house and letting the storm door on the back porch bang shut behind her. This was the first football game of the season, and Sara's old irritation swept over her, catching her by surprise. She went to her room and closed the door. It was as if Sara were trying to put as many closed doors between her and the football game as she could manage.

"Geez," Sara said out loud to herself. "What is my problem?"

Sara had no use whatsoever for football season. It wasn't uncommon for most of the town to turn out for these Friday-evening games, and many of them even traveled to other cities when the team had an away game. Sara never went to the game, no matter where it was played. She tossed a book onto her bed and flopped down on her stomach, turning the pages. She had no interest in this book either.

Sara wished she could go to the river and swing from the tree; she wanted relief from this fidgety, irritable feeling. She knew it wasn't a good idea to wander through the woods at night, but the thought of swinging from the tree in the dark did make her feel a little better. *The sky is so light,* Sara thought. *Maybe it won't be too dark.*

She opened her bedroom door and found her mother still in the kitchen, tidying up after dinner.

"I'll finish up here, Mom."

"Oh, thank you, honey. Janet's saving seats for us, so we don't have to rush. Why don't you come with us, Sara? It'll be fun."

"No, I have some things I need to work on for school," Sara said. (That's one good thing about school—homework was always a believable alibi. It could be stretched to encompass an entire weekend, or it could shrink to nothing at all; and her parents, for some strange reason, never seemed to question it.)

Sara went back into her room, now eager for her family to leave for the football game. The idea of going to the thicket and having this strange new experience of swinging from the tree in the darkness was feeling more and more like a great adventure.

Sara opened her bottom drawer, digging deep to the bottom, searching for her long underwear. She smiled as she thought about how funny she felt wearing these, but she had to admit, they did make a leisurely afternoon of playing in the snow much more pleasant.

Sara waited until she heard her family's final "See ya later, Sara," and the loud squeak of the big metal garage door sliding open before she took the underwear from her drawer and pulled them onto her body. She giggled as she looked at herself in the mirror, turning around to examine the trap door in the backside. "Who makes these things?" She giggled. "Can you imagine what people would say about me if they knew I was swinging from trees in the middle of the night wearing *these?*"

Sara finished dressing, grabbed her coat and hat and gloves, and headed out the back door. As she walked, her irritation lifted, and her usual eagerness for life returned.

I'll cut through the field, Sara decided. *Half the town will offer me a ride to the ball game if I walk on the road!*

It had seemed so bright while she was out in the open pasture, but as Sara ducked onto the trail and walked deeper into the woods, she could barely see anything at all.

It felt eerie to be out in the dark all alone. "What was I thinking?" Sara said under her breath, wishing that she had thought to bring a flashlight. She turned around and looked back at the dark trail she'd just traveled and then ahead to the even darker trail before her. Neither direction was a comfortable choice; she felt paralyzed with indecision. The harder she tried to see, the darker everything seemed. And then Sara heard a sound coming from the direction of the tree house. It was the familiar sound of someone swinging from the tree.

Her indecision lifted instantly and she began to walk toward the tree house. It was no lighter now than before, but Sara had no trouble moving quickly down the path. As she came out into the opening at the river, she saw a form swinging out over the river. She heard a thud and then Seth's voice saying, "Yes, just right!"

"Seth?" Sara called out, happy to realize it was him and surprised to find him here in the dark. "Is that you?"

"Geez, Sara, you scared me to death," Seth called back. "What are you doing here? I thought you'd be at the ball game."

"Nah," Sara answered, not wanting to try to explain to Seth how she felt about such things. "I never go."

"Me neither," Seth answered easily.

"Why not?" Sara embarrassed herself with her quick and prying response. She really didn't like it when others pressed her with questions about her decisions, and here she was doing just that to Seth. But he didn't seem to mind.

"Oh, I don't know. I never really felt a part of any school. When I'd see a great run or pass or block, I'd cheer. But I got in trouble over and over again, 'cause half the time they were on the wrong team. I just got tired of it."

Sara was fascinated. Seth had pinpointed exactly what had bothered her about the ball games: She didn't like the feeling that she had to approve of everything her team did just because it was *her* team, and she didn't like the idea that she had to disapprove of everything the *other* team did, no matter what, just because it was the other team. Sara didn't know anyone else who felt the way she did about ball games. She felt so happy to have Seth as her friend.

"How long you been out here?" Sara asked.

"Since about dark," Seth answered.

"Aren't you cold?"

"Nah, I've got on . . ." Seth stopped in the middle of his sentence. He really didn't want to tell Sara about his thermal underwear. He felt silly enough putting them on. He hoped she hadn't heard him.

But Sara *had* heard, and now she started laughing.

Her laughing was contagious, and he began laughing, too.

"Are they red?" Sara whispered.

Seth laughed hard. "Yeah, how'd you know?"

"Oh, I don't know," Sara laughed. "Just a wild guess. Seth, we are friends of a feather . . . game-dodging, tree-swinging, red-flanneled friends of a feather."

They laughed so hard that tears filled their eyes. It felt good to be so completely understood by another. It felt really good.

CHAPTER 14

Searching for Caves

Sara found Seth's note in her school locker: *Sara, I'll see you at the tree house. But don't go up until I get there. I've got a surprise.*

Sara waited at the base of the tree. She deliberately didn't look up into the tree because she didn't want to spoil his surprise.

Seth blasted through the bushes. "You didn't go up, did you?"

"I wanted to, but I waited for you. What's the surprise?"

"You go up. I'll be right there," Seth said. He had a paper bag under his arm and an unusual twinkle in his eye.

Sara climbed the ladder and Seth was soon behind her. They sat perched in the tree house. Sara looked around. "Okay, I'm ready." She couldn't see anything different.

"Okay, close your eyes."

Sara closed her eyes and Seth untied a rope that was hidden behind the tree. He put the rope in her hands and said, "Okay, now hold on to this tight and open your eyes."

Sara opened her eyes and laughed. "What in the world?"

"Don't let go. Just pull gently on the rope."

Seth had tied some pulleys to the upper branches and had threaded a long thin rope through them. As Sara pulled on the rope, up came a large bucket filled with a bottle of water, some candy bars, paper cups, Sara's very heavy book bag, and some plastic trash bags.

"It's a lot easier to pull this stuff up after we get up here than to carry it up the ladder," Seth said, fishing for a compliment from Sara.

"It's ingenious! I love it! Where did you get the ropes and the pulleys?"

"The gym teacher gave them to me. He said they'd been in the equipment room in a box for years, and he was just going to throw them out."

Sara smiled. She'd noticed how often people eagerly opened up to Seth. She had never known anyone like him. He just seemed to bring out the best in people, and they often extended themselves in ways she hadn't seen them do before. This gym coach was seen by most as a very strict, usually unpleasant, grump. And yet here he was giving Seth just what he wanted to make their secret hideaway even more perfect. *I guess everyone likes Seth,* Sara thought.

"Where do you come up with these ideas?" Sara asked.

"Oh, I don't know, I guess I've just had lots of hideouts."

"How many? Tell me about some of them."

"Oh, I don't know." Seth was embarrassed. None of them had been very exciting, none of them had been as great as this one, and none of them had he ever shared with a girl before. Usually, he shared them with no one. His little brother had found out about one or two of them, but Seth hadn't intended that. A hideaway is a very private thing.

Sara's eyes were sparkling as she tried to imagine all the wonderful places Seth had lived and all of the wonderful hideaways he had created out in the woods. Seth saw her look of great expectation. He grinned as he felt her prodding him for details, and he certainly didn't want to disappoint her. He knew Sara would never see his old hideaways. He knew he wouldn't likely see any of them again either; and he considered, for a moment, offering a grander version of them than they really were, wanting his stories to match up with Sara's expectation. But exaggeration was not Seth's style. In fact, he was more likely to play down his creativity than to exaggerate it. But there was something more. In the short time he and Sara had been meeting and swinging and laughing and playing and talking, he had come to trust her in a way he had never trusted any other. He didn't want to do anything to mess that up.

Sara pulled her knees up to her chest and waited. Seth grinned. It was impossible to deny her.

"Well, they weren't that great, Sara. Mostly just places that I could go off by myself; most of them had to be close by, and I never got to spend much time in any of them. But it felt good just knowing that they were there."

"Yeah," Sara said. "I know what you mean."

"The first one I found by accident. It was on the back side of our neighbor's property. He had a big place, I mean, like hundreds of acres, and way back away from the house and away from any of the pastures and barns, I found a tree house."

"Wow!" Sara said. "Was it nice, like this one?"

Seth laughed. "It was a lot bigger than this one. It was in a grove of trees, and the floor of it was connected to three different trees. I don't know who built it, I never saw anyone else near it, and I never told anyone about it. I hated to leave that place, but we only lived there for about six months. I suppose that big old tree house is just sitting there rotting."

"What else?"

"Then we moved to a place near a farm that had lots of barns and sheds. They raised pigs and milk cows. The barns were all connected with fences and corrals, and it was a fun place to be because you could go from barn to barn, walking on fences and rooftops, and your feet never had to touch the ground. They kept bales of hay in two of the big barns. It was fun to rearrange the bales; they made great walls. That was a fun place. I never told anyone about that place, either. It was just me and a few cats who hung around to find mice."

"Then what?" Sara was enjoying her mental pictures of all of these neat places.

"A few of them were caves. The caves were great. Sometimes a little creepy 'cause you never know who else lives in there with you, but I never saw anything very scary."

"Caves? Hmm. We don't have any caves around here."

"Oh, sure you do. There are probably lots of caves up in the hills."

"Really!?" Sara was surprised. "I guess just because I haven't seen them doesn't mean they aren't there. Do you think we could find one?"

"Yeah, we probably could," Seth said hesitantly, worried about the time it would take just to get to the foothills.

"I'd *love* to find a cave." Sara's eyes were bright with excitement. "Please, Seth, say yes."

"Okay." Seth smiled. "We'll find a cave. But I don't think we'll be able to go there very often."

"Oh, I know," Sara said excitedly. "We don't have to go there much. I just want to *find* one."

Seth knew that his father was always irritated if he came home late. While there weren't as many family chores to do here as there had been in other places they had lived, his parents still expected Seth to do his part in helping out. And even when there wasn't that much that needed to be done, his parents always managed to find something for Seth and his brother to do.

"I don't know, Sara, it would take several hours. I'm not sure . . ."

"We could cut school," Sara said.

Seth smiled. "Yeah, we could."

"No one would know; I never miss school," Sara said. "No one would suspect anything. Come on, Seth, it'll be fun. Please!"

The idea of having a whole day to explore and visit with Sara was enticing. There was nothing that Seth longed for more than the freedom to do what he wanted to do.

"I hope you know what you're doing. Okay, when shall we go?"

"Next week. Let's go on Tuesday!"

Sara felt so happy. The idea of a whole day exploring for caves sounded so delicious. She stood up, grabbed hold of the swinging rope, and without even putting her foot in the loop, leaped into the air, swinging out over the river.

"Geez, Sara," Seth said under his breath, almost afraid to look, fearing that she wouldn't be able to hold on and would fall into the river.

But Sara had a firm grip on the rope, and as she swung out over the river, she beamed. She couldn't remember ever feeling better. *All truly is well,* she thought. She felt for the right timing to leap from the rope and landed another perfect dismount.

Sara stood on the bank and watched as Seth pulled the rope up into the tree. He gathered the candy wrappers and Sara's jacket and book bag and put them into the bucket and carefully lowered it down. Then, as Sara watched from below, he leaped into the air out across the river. He, too, had a perfect landing and glanced at Sara as he landed. They beamed at each other, remembering the first several disastrous landings. They had both come a long way in a short time. They went back to the tree, raised the empty bucket back up into it, and tied the rope to a nail on the back side of the trunk. They felt lucky that no one had yet discovered their wonderful hideaway.

"Seth, this is such a great tree house!"

Seth grinned.

CHAPTER 15

Saved by an Owl

Sara awakened and immediately felt exhilarated. It was Tuesday, and this was the day she and Seth had agreed to meet at the tree house. Today they would explore the foothills looking for caves.

Sara's mother was busy in the kitchen. "What's up, Sara?" her mother asked as Sara entered the room.

"What do you mean?" Sara asked. What an odd thing for her mother to ask. Sara looked away, not wanting to look her mother in the eyes.

"Well, you're up early, aren't you?" her mother replied.

"Oh, yeah, I guess I am," Sara said with relief. "I needed to use the bathroom," she said, justifying her white lie with the fact that she really did have to go now. Sara hadn't imagined an overly interested mother on the day of her great escape.

"Well, if you have extra time, I could use some help in here, dear."

Sara hadn't planned on that either.

"Okay," Sara said, "I'll be out in a minute."

What is it with parents? Sara thought. *They always seem to sense when there's something exciting that you want to do, and then they have some boring chore that turns up that spoils things.*

Sara took her bath and stood in front of her closet trying to decide what to wear. *It has to look like I'm going to school,* she thought, *and old enough so that if it gets torn or something, it won't matter. And something that won't stand out.*

"Green is good," Sara muttered as she chose a jumper that she hadn't worn since last year and pulled it on. It wasn't as loose fitting as she would have liked. She'd grown some since then, but it seemed like the best choice. Sara pulled her hair back into a ponytail and joined her mother in the kitchen.

"You look nice today," her mother said. "I haven't seen you wear that jumper in a long time."

Geez, Sara thought. *What is it? I must be wearing a sign that says, "Notice me! I'm doing something sneaky today!"*

Sara washed two dozen canning jars while her mother peeled and cored apples. "If I let these go any longer, they won't be good," her mother said.

Sara didn't answer. She was deep in thought, wondering if she and Seth would find a cave today.

"Okay, Sara, that's all I need. Thanks, honey. You'd better get going."

"Oh, yeah," Sara answered. "I'd better go."

Her mother watched her, smiling, enjoying the different moods of her fast-growing daughter.

Sara and Seth had planned to go to school for the first hour or two. Each of them would then leave, "not feeling well," and then they'd meet at the swinging tree. No one would think anything of seeing either of them walking in that direction since that was the way they would normally go home. Then they'd walk up the riverbank where it was unlikely they would see anyone until they could get back past the school. Once there, they could take any number of walking trails up the hill, past the junk yard, past the old grist mill that hadn't been running in Sara's lifetime, and into the hills above town. If they stayed off the highway, no one would notice them.

The second bell rang as Sara made her way to Mr. Marchant's office. "Mr. Marchant, I'd like to go home. I'm not feeling well," Sara lied to her principal.

"I'm sorry to hear that, Sara. Do you want me to call your mother?"

"No, that's all right. I don't have a long walk.

And I don't want to bother her at work. I'll call her when I get home."

"Well, all right. You take it easy today."

Sara walked out of the school, both elated and embarrassed. It was only because she was known as a really good kid that she was getting away with this. It felt odd to be riding on a reputation for being good while you were being so very bad, but her enthusiasm for the exciting day ahead overrode her momentary feeling of conscience as Sara walked toward home.

And, just as she had imagined, no one else spoke to her, no one offered her a ride; no one seemed to notice her at all.

She climbed the ladder on the swinging tree and had barely sat down when Seth came blasting through the bushes. She laughed when she saw him in his dark green shirt and faded jeans. She knew he'd chosen a careful camouflage, too.

He climbed the tree, grinning from ear to ear. It seemed they had both gotten away with it, and this day belonged entirely to them. This time felt better than treasure to both of them, but especially to Seth.

Seth opened the lid on the bench seat and pulled out two well-worn pairs of fishing boots. "They're big," he said, "but they'll keep our feet dry as we walk up the river."

"Where in the world did you get these?"

"They're my dad's," Seth said. "I brought them over last night. He'd kill me if he knew I took them, but he won't be looking for them today, and they'll help us get out of town."

Sara smiled, but felt a twinge of discomfort in her stomach. The plot was thickening as the white lies turned to true lies and now to stealing, or at least some pretty heavy borrowing. She could tell by Seth's demeanor that he wasn't kidding about being in big trouble if his father found out about the boots. She shuddered to imagine how he would feel about the tree house or cutting school.

"Hey, Sara, this is going to be fun. Don't worry. No one will know."

Sara brightened. "You're right. Let's go."

They lowered their jackets and the fishing boots down from the tree in the bucket, climbed down themselves, and then pulled the empty bucket back up into the tree. Sara pulled on her big floppy boots. She squealed a little as she pulled the boot up her leg; it was cold inside and felt slimy. Seth pulled on his boots, and off they went.

"Let's stay on the riverbank as much as we can. We'll only wade when we have to."

"That's fine by me," Sara said.

They walked slowly up the bank of the river, tromping through deep grass and ducking under branches. Seth walked ahead, doing his best to forge a trail for Sara. He accidentally let go of a branch too soon, and it flapped Sara in the face. She laughed out loud, and Seth laughed, too.

A large bird flushed up from the bushes and flew up into the sky. "Hey," Seth said, "that looks like an owl. Sara, do you think that's *your* owl?"

"That's not him."

"How do you know?" Seth asked. "How can you tell for sure that it's not the same owl?"

"Because my owl's dead!" Sara blurted.

She felt embarrassed that she had reacted so strongly. "Well, I mean, he's not really dead, because . . ." Sara stopped. She wasn't really ready to try to explain to Seth everything that she'd come to know about death, and that death really isn't like what most everybody thinks it is.

"Billy and Jason shot him . . . in the thicket . . . he died in my arms on Thacker's Trail."

Seth was quiet. He was sorry he'd asked the question. It was clear that Sara had experienced real trauma over the death of this owl. And then it hit him: *He must have died right on that same spot on Thacker's Trail where I was faking my death! No wonder Sara was so upset that day!*

Sara wiped a tear from her face. She was embarrassed to have Seth see her cry, and she was even more embarrassed that she was still bothered by Solomon's death.

At that moment, the owl flew out across the

river and then back toward the swinging tree; he flew up into the tree and perched on the platform that Seth had built, and looked up the river in the direction of Seth and Sara.

"Hey, he's in our tree house," Seth said.

"Yeah," Sara said softly. "He *is.*"

Sara remembered Solomon's dying words to her: *It is with great joy that I released that physical body, knowing that whenever I want to, I can pour my energy into another, younger, stronger, faster . . .*

Sara squinted her eyes, trying to focus on the owl. The owl flew from the tree, following the identical trajectory of Seth and Sara's swing on the rope, and then soared high up into the sky and out of view . . . *Solomon!* Sara thought. *Is that you?*

Sara felt such a pang of excitement she could barely breathe. Was it possible that Solomon had decided to come back to be with her on Thacker's Trail? And if it *were* him, why hadn't he told her he was coming? *Solomon,* Sara called out for him in her mind. No answer came back. Sara had been so involved with Seth lately that she hadn't been talking much with Solomon. In fact, Sara could barely remember her last talk with her dearly departed friend.

"I guess we're going to have to wade here," Seth said.

His voice jolted Sara's awareness back into her now, and she followed Seth's lead as he gingerly waded out into the shallow water on the river's edge. The river was wide here, and the current wasn't swift, so they should have no problem walking around this clump of trees and dense underbrush. Sara looked back at the thick bushes and wondered, for the first time, if maybe they were making a mistake. She worried that they might come to other places like this where the trees were *not* passable and the river might not be, *either,* but Seth seemed confident enough, so she followed quietly along.

It was hard work, plodding along in the big boots. Sara wished they had chosen a different path. She was beginning to feel tired and was glad Seth was carrying the heavy backpack with the water bottle and fruit and candy they'd stashed inside.

"There's a clear spot up ahead," Seth called out. "We'll stop and rest there."

Sara smiled. Seth was reading her mind again. "I brought some candy bars," he said. "Let's stop and eat them."

That sounded good to Sara.

"How far do you think we've come?" Sara asked.

"Not very far," Seth said. "Look, out there, isn't that the top of the gas-station sign?"

"Oh, geez," Sara muttered. It was truly discouraging to see what a short distance they had traveled. The gas station wasn't anywhere near the edge of town.

"This is slow going," Sara said. "I wish we could just go out on the street and walk. This sneaking around is hard work."

Seth laughed. "Let's follow the river a little more, and then we'll take off through the pasture behind the graveyard. I don't think anybody in *there* will tell on us."

"Don't bet on it." Sara laughed. She had a new respect for the dead. It turns out that they aren't as dead as she always thought they were. Then she again thought of Solomon.

They finished their candy, drank some water, pulled the big boots back on, and continued their upstream trek. And before long, just as Seth had guessed, the stream made a sharp turn and straight ahead lay the cemetery. "How many dead people are *in* there, do you think?" Seth asked.

"I think *all* of them," Sara kidded.

"Sara," Seth groaned.

Sara giggled. "Well, some old jokes are worth digging up over and over again, don't you think?"

Seth groaned again.

"Some jokes just seem to take on a life of their own."

"Sara, stop, I'm *begging* you."

"Some jokes just seem to live forever." Sara laughed.

"Sara, I'm *dying* here. Please, *stop!*"

Sara laughed. Seth laughed, too.

"There's some real neat old headstones in there. Wanna go see?" Sara asked.

"Nah. Not today. Maybe later. We better keep moving if we're going to find any caves."

Sara was relieved. She never liked going in the graveyard. It always felt weird. Not because of the dead people, but because the visiting adults seemed sad and depressed there. Sara's views on death had changed dramatically, thanks to Solomon, but she could feel, especially when they visited the graveyard, that most people had serious issues about death.

"Hey, Sara, look, there's that owl again."

Sara looked out into the graveyard, and on top of the tallest monument . . . in fact, the only monument in the graveyard, was the owl. He sat there like a statue, like he was part of the monument, too.

"It's like he's following us," Seth said, surprised.

"Yeah, it does seem like that," Sara agreed, and when she looked back, the owl wasn't there.

"Did he fly away?" she asked.

"I didn't see where he went. Ready to go?" Seth asked, not nearly as interested in the owl as Sara was. "Give me your boots, Sara. I'll carry them." He tied them together and draped them over his shoulder with his own. Sara felt relieved.

"Do you think we'll come back this same way?" Sara asked.

"Most likely. But sometimes when you get up high on the hillside, you can see a better trail back. Why?"

"I just thought maybe we could stash the boots here and then pick them up on the way back. They're so heavy, and don't tell your father I said so, but they're smelly, too."

Seth laughed. "Your secret is safe with me, Sara. That's a good idea." Seth looked around for a place to leave the boots. "Let's check out that old tree up ahead!" Sure enough, just as Seth had guessed, the tree had a big hollow on the back side.

"What makes a big old tree like this die, anyway?" Sara asked.

"Oh, I don't know, lots of things, I guess," Seth said. "This one looks to me like it was struck by lightning."

"Hmm," Sara muttered. She didn't know lightning had ever struck near here.

"Sometimes they get diseased and die, and sometimes they just get old. Nothin' lives forever, you know."

"That's what they *say*," Sara said.

Seth stuffed the boots into the hole in the back of the tree, and off they went. They crawled under and through an occasional fence from one farmer's pasture to another, happy that, in over two hours of walking, they hadn't encountered anyone. Except for the owl.

"How do you know where to look?" Sara asked. She was beginning to wonder if this whole cave thing was such a good idea. She hadn't realized it would be such a long walk.

"See those rock cliffs up there?" Seth pointed off toward the hillsides. "See that bank of trees, there?"

"Yes, I see that."

"See that dark spot just above them? I think that's a cave. Can't tell for sure, but I've seen lots of cliffs, and those cliffs look to me like they have caves."

"Okay." Sara smiled. "I hope you're right. How much farther do you think it is?"

"Not far. We'll be there in less than an hour. Do you want to rest again?"

"No, I'm fine. Just wondered."

They trudged silently along, not talking much to each other. *Funny,* Sara thought, *I thought this would be a lot more fun than it is.* She hadn't expected it to take so long, and she hadn't expected to get so tired. It was a much steeper climb now, and her little toe was beginning to hurt. Sara wanted to stop and take off her shoe and straighten her sock, which felt bunched up and uncomfortable. *Geez, am I trouble or what? I'll bet Seth won't be cutting class with a girl again anytime soon.*

"Let's sit here for a while, Sara. If we stop and rest and eat and drink often, we'll keep up our stamina better."

"Oh, good," Sara said, tugging off her shoe. What sweet relief! She pulled off her sock and pulled it back on again. *Much better,* she thought.

Seth smiled as he tossed her an apple. His toss was quick and accurate, and Sara looked up quickly and snatched the apple out of the air with her left hand.

They both laughed.

They finished the apples, and now feeling refreshed and eager, they continued on. "You know," Sara said, "this really is a beautiful day." She had gotten her second wind, her guilt had subsided, and right before them was the cliff they had seen from the pasture below.

"Uh-oh," Sara said, as she saw the very dense underbrush all along the cliff row. "Now what?"

"Wait here," Seth said. "I'll go see if I can find an easier way through this."

Sara really didn't want to stay there by herself, but she didn't like the idea of getting all scratched up either.

"Okay," she said reluctantly.

"If I don't find something fast, I'll come right back," Seth called as he disappeared into the bushes.

"Good," Sara said to herself, sitting on a rock ledge clutching her knees and looking back down at the valley. She had become interested in seeing if she could identify landmarks down in the valley, when Seth came back through the bushes.

"Come on, Sara, you're gonna *love* this one. This is one of the best caves I've ever seen!"

"Really?"

"Yeah, it's great! It's kinda hard to get through this part, but then it's a clear path," Seth said, as he pulled the bushes back so Sara could enter. They walked a hundred yards or so, and then right before them was an entrance to a great big cave.

"Wow!" Sara said. "I can't believe that every kid in town hasn't found this."

"Well, from the markings on the walls inside I'd say we aren't the first ones here, but we're the only ones here today, or anytime lately. I don't think anybody's been in here for years. Look how faded the writing is."

Seth and Sara stood inside the entry. "I can't believe this," Sara said. "This is a big place!"

The entrance to the cave was about five feet in diameter, but once through that opening, the cave opened up. The ceiling of the cave looked like it was at least 20 feet tall, and all over the walls and even the ceiling of that first big room were painted, in truly untalented fashion, names and stick figures—and even a happy face.

"Whoever painted this has about as much artistic talent as I do," Sara said, laughing.

"Yeah, and not much respect for natural beauty, either," Seth said. Sara could tell that Seth didn't appreciate the defacing of this beautiful cave.

"Wanna go farther back in?" Sara asked, wanting to see more and at the same time really hoping that Seth would say, "Later" or "Next time" or "No, I really don't want to go farther."

"Yeah," Seth said. Seth sounded as if he genuinely wanted to see more. His enthusiasm boosted her courage some, but she still felt strong reluctance to trudge forward into this dark, unknown territory. She certainly didn't want to be a party pooper, but with every step they moved forward, Sara felt stronger and stronger resistance to taking the next step.

Seth wasn't hurrying either. He was very proud of himself for producing a cave so quickly and easily for his new friend, but he was also feeling reluctance about bolting into this dark unknown. But he wasn't about to disappoint Sara. After all, they had come this far.

Seth took off his backpack and pulled out the flashlight he'd stashed. It was an old one that didn't put out much of a beam, but it was much better than nothing, and he shined his dim light back into the cave. "Geez," he said, "this cave goes on *forever!*" His light wasn't strong enough to find the back wall of the cave. "Sara, I've never seen a cave like this. This is awesome!"

Those words weren't particularly reassuring to Sara. She would have preferred words more like "Yes, Sara, I've explored many caves exactly like this one, and they are always the same: safe, empty of anything scary, and really fun to explore." But she could hear from Seth's tones that he was feeling as uneasy about this cave as she was.

Seth shined the dim light around, looking up to find the ceiling and out to find the back walls of the cave, but the light just couldn't seem to find the top or the back of this huge space. Seth pointed the light back down at the floor—and then he stopped dead in his tracks. "Shusssh," he said softly. "Don't move."

Sara stood frozen. What did Seth see?

Then, suddenly, there was a commotion of fluttering and dust, and Sara heard Seth's voice saying, "What the heck . . ."

He wheeled around looking back at the cave entrance past Sara's startled face and yelled, "Look, Sara, it's the owl! It's the *owl!*"

Sara and Seth ran back to the cave entrance in time to see this very large owl flying with a very large snake hanging from his beak.

"Sara!" Seth shouted, "That owl saved us! That

snake was coiled ready to strike. If the owl hadn't been there, it woulda had me for sure!"

"Let's get out of here!" Sara exclaimed, running out of the cave, and Seth was right behind her. Sara had no trouble making her way through the brush and down the rocky ledge back to the pasture. She didn't even stop to look back to see if Seth was still behind her until she was back in the pasture and ready to cross under the first fence.

"I thought you said you weren't afraid of snakes," Seth said, grinning.

"I changed my mind," Sara retorted, out of breath. "And I've changed my mind about caves, too."

Seth laughed. "Yeah, me, too. At least for now. But that's an awesome cave, Sara. Usually snakes don't bother you. They usually get out of your way. I guess we just surprised it. Hey, what about that *owl?* Do you believe that?"

"Well, yes, I guess I do." (Oh, there was so much to tell Seth.)

"We'd better head back," Seth told her, looking at his watch. "Time flies when you're having fun."

"Yeah, or something like that."

It was much easier walking back down into the valley than it had been to walk up out of it, and Sara and Seth had a new energy that was propelling them as well. Sara appreciated that Seth seemed to hold his pace to one that was so comfortable for her, and Seth was glad that Sara was able to easily keep up with him. They visited, walked, and sometimes ran down out of the foothills.

"These old fences don't seem like they hold much in," Seth said, as he put his foot on one wire holding it down, and pulled on the top wire holding it up, making a wide enough opening that Sara could slip through. Once on the other side, Sara did the same for him. "Yeah, lucky for us." Sara laughed.

They happily made their way through the pastures and back to the old dead tree where they had stashed the fishing boots. As they approached the tree, Sara felt reluctance. She really dreaded the idea of putting on those smelly old boots. And the idea of wading back down the river wasn't the least bit appealing either. Seth felt it, too. Sara didn't say what she was feeling; she waited as Seth climbed up the back side of the tree and watched as he reached inside.

"Ya know, Sara, school will be letting out in a few minutes. We could walk right past the school and blend in with everyone else as they're heading home. What do ya think? Are you willing to try it?"

"Yeah," Sara said excitedly. She liked that idea a whole lot better than trudging down the river. And a game of hide-and-seek, or at least a game of, "I'm invisible and you won't notice me," was exciting.

"I'll come back later and get the boots."

Sara felt such relief. "Well, then, let's get going!" she said gladly, perfectly happy to leave those smelly old boots behind.

As they crossed through the last pasture above the school yard, they could see that it was empty. No one was moving about. Then the bell rang, the doors burst open, and the school yard and parking lots filled with students and teachers, spilling out of the buildings like prisoners who had just made their escape. Sara felt a twinge of discomfort, or maybe it was excitement—or maybe it was guilt. It was hard to pinpoint exactly *what* she was feeling as she saw fellow students leaving school at the end of a long day, just as she knew she should have been doing at this moment as well.

"Okay," Seth said, "I'll go out ahead. We shouldn't go together."

"Okay. Ya want to meet back at the tree house?"

"Yeah, I'll see ya there." Seth took off in the direction of the school.

Sara watched Seth until he disappeared behind the building. She tied her shoelace; tucked her shirt in; pulled the rubber band out of her hair; and ran her fingers through her long, curly hair to bring it to some order. She laughed as she found a good-sized twig tangled in her curls. "Oh, *that's* nice, how long has that been in there?" she said aloud, feeling self-conscious about her appearance. She put the rubber band back in her hair and followed Seth past the school.

Mr. Marchant came out of the building just as Sara rounded the corner. He looked at Sara and waved.

Sara's heart stopped. *Uh-oh,* she thought.

But Mr. Marchant got into his car, backed out of his parking place, and rounded the corner.

Either he didn't see me; he forgot I went home sick; we all look alike to him; or I'm in big, big trouble and he's toying with me. Sara's mouth felt dry, and suddenly she felt very hot. "Oh well," Sara said, "what's done is done."

Sara walked quickly toward the swinging tree. She felt more conspicuous than she had ever felt in her life. "I'd probably glow in the dark," she muttered under her breath.

In all of her life, Sara couldn't remember living through such a topsy-turvy day. It had begun with such promise. A whole day to escape and explore with her best friend. But it hadn't been anything like she thought it would be. It was very hard work wading up the river, and the smelly boots didn't add much to the pleasure of the day either. Finding the cave was great, but getting chased out of it by a big, mean snake was truly terrifying. Being saved by the owl was incredible! But then, getting spotted by Mr. Marchant . . . well, if there could have been a worse ending to the day, Sara couldn't imagine *what* it would be.

CHAPTER 16

Follow Your Heart

Sara ran almost all the way from the school grounds to Thacker's Trail. She ducked off the road into the bushes and half walked, half ran to the tree house. She was eager to talk with Seth and tell him how she had been spotted by the school principal. Of all the people in the world to see her, why did it have to be the one person she had lied to?

"Hey, Seth!" Sara called out.

No answer came back.

"He should've been here way before now," Sara said out loud.

"Seth!" She called out again, hoping that her voice would somehow reach out to where her eyes couldn't see, and find him.

Sara sat on the floor of the tree house, pulled her legs up against her chest, and rested her chin on her knees. She was absolutely exhausted.

"Solomon?" Sara said, quietly. "Can you hear me?"

I can, indeed, Sara. It's nice to have an opportunity to visit. What is it you want to talk about?

Sara closed her eyes and got comfortable. She had learned, through much practice, that if she really had something important that she wanted to talk about, that she could hear Solomon's words in her mind as clearly as her portable radio and earphones played music into her ears. Sara had so much she wanted to talk with Solomon about.

"Solomon, where *is* Seth? He should have been here by now. Do you think he got caught? Do you think he's in trouble? He's probably in as much trouble as I am. Oh, Solomon, why did we ever decide to skip school?"

Solomon listened while Sara poured out her worry. When she finally stopped, Solomon began. *Well, Sara, I'm sure that it's not as bad as all of that. Don't make too much of all of this.*

"But, Solomon, Mr. Marchant saw me coming back onto the school grounds. Do you think he remembered that I said that I was going home sick today?"

Well, Sara, that is a possibility.

"Do you think he recognized me?"

That is most likely, Sara. You are one of his favorite students. I don't think he would forget who you are.

"That's just *great,* Solomon. I'm one of his

favorite students, and now I'm in big trouble."

What makes you so sure you are in trouble, Sara?

"I can feel it. I feel awful. I wish we'd just gone to school today like we were supposed to. I guess I'm really a bad person, Solomon. Are *you* mad at me?"

Sara, there is nothing that you could do that would cause me to be mad at you. My love for you is not dependent upon your behavior. My love for you is constant.

Sara appreciated Solomon's loving words, but she certainly didn't feel that she deserved them.

"You mean, no matter how bad I am, you still love me?"

Solomon smiled. *Sara, I do not believe that you could ever be bad.*

"Hmm." Sara felt confused. She had never known anyone like Solomon.

Sara, I would not want you to alter your behavior in order to gain my approval. I would actually prefer that you seek to find harmony with your own guidance system that comes forth from within you. I want you to make your decisions based upon how they feel to you, not because you are worried about what I might think.

Sara was beginning to feel a little better. It was comforting that her dear Solomon had not lost faith in her.

I have noticed, Sara, that good intentions are usually at the basis of most deception.

"What do you mean?"

Why did you want to keep your cave exploration a secret? Why didn't you want your parents or Mr. Marchant to know about it?

"Because they'd be mad at me if they knew."

Is it important to you that they love you?

"Yes."

You found yourself in an uncomfortable position, Sara. You want them to love you, but you also wanted to explore for caves. By not telling them your plans, you were attempting to satisfy both intentions at the same time.

You see, Sara, if there is only one person that you are attempting to please, in time, with enough effort, you may be able to stand on your head in enough different ways to please him or her. But if there are two different people, or three, or more, it very quickly becomes far too much to juggle. The only real alternative is for you to discover your own guidance system that comes forth from within you. In short, Sara—you just have to follow your own heart.

Sara was beginning to feel a little better.

No one else can really know what the best choices are for you. You are the only one who can really know that.

"Sure seems like there are a lot of people who think they know better."

They mean well, Sara. Most have your best interests in mind when they try to guide you. But remember: The

Law of Attraction is really behind everything that comes to you or happens to you. And so, if you are a vibrational match to good things, then only good things can come to you.

Nothing so terrible has happened. I am rather happy that the two of you had such an interesting day. Much more value will come to you from this cave exploration experience than if you had been at your school all day.

"So you think it's okay that I skipped school today? And that I lied to Mr. Marchant?"

Well, let's see, Sara, let's check it with your own guidance system. How did you feel when you told Mr. Marchant you were going home sick?

"Hmm. I didn't feel very good *then*. I felt guilty. It bothered me that he trusted me."

So your guidance was telling you that this action was not a match to your desire to be trusted.

When you thought about a day of skipping school and exploring for caves, how did you feel?

"I felt *great*, Solomon. I felt happy and excited."

Good, then your guidance was telling you, this is a good idea.

"But Solomon, I don't understand. How could I get what I *did* want, like exploring for caves, without doing something that I *didn't* want, like lying?"

Before I answer that, Sara, let me ask you some questions. How was your day of exploring? Was it

107

glorious? Was it fun? Was it wonderful? Was it a perfect day?

"Well, some of it was wonderful. Sometimes I felt really, really good, but some of it was hard, some of it was scary. It was sort of a mixture."

Actually, Sara, your day was a perfect match to the way you were feeling about it. You felt both good about it and bad about it, and the day was a perfect match to the way you were feeling.

"Are you saying that if I had felt only good about this day of exploring, that the day would have turned out only good?"

That's exactly right, Sara. The <u>Law of Attraction</u> is always exact.

"So I didn't have to tell a lie to get to go?"

That's right. Once the two of you decided that you wanted to explore for caves, you could have held that idea, purely, and a way for that to happen, without violating any other desires, would have opened for you. In fact, Sara, it is never too late to find a good-feeling place about anything—things will constantly change to match the feeling you have inside.

"You mean, if I find a good-feeling place now, I could still keep Mr. Marchant from being disappointed in me?"

Yes, indeed. You have only to think of him understanding you, and loving you. Remember, Sara, you can tell by the way you are feeling, how you are doing. If your thought feels good, then good things are coming to you.

Try to find thoughts that feel good.

"Okay, Solomon. I'll work on that. I better get going. I hope everything is all right with Seth."

Imagine that all is well.

"Okay. Thanks for your help."

CHAPTER 17

Are These Good Kids?

S ara lay in her bed thinking about Mr. Marchant. She had a knot in her stomach, and a very
strong feeling of fear was pulsing through her.

"I'd give anything if I didn't have to go to
school today," she said, right out loud.

*If your thought feels good, then good things are com-
ing to you.* Sara remembered Solomon's words.

It was hard to find a thought that felt good.
Worrisome images about why Seth hadn't been at
the tree house, what Mr. Marchant must be thinking of her, and what her parents would do if they
found out seemed to dominate Sara's thoughts.

Solomon's words came into Sara's mind: *Sara,
it's never too late to find a good-feeling place about
anything—things will constantly change to match the
feeling you have inside.*

Sara sat up in bed and took a pen and notebook
from the table beside her bed. She began to make

a list of things that always made her feel good. And in big letters at the top of her page she wrote: TREE HOUSE

She smiled. Thinking of the tree house always made Sara feel good. Then she wrote more:

THE LADDER TO THE TREE HOUSE
THE SWINGING ROPE
SETH'S PULLEYS AND THE BUCKET

Sara thought of how excited Seth had been to show her the tree house, and how thrilled she had been to discover it. She remembered how exhilarating her first swing out over the river had been, and she laughed as she remembered her first muddy dismount from the rope. And as she thought of the day Seth showed her the pulleys and the bucket and of the night they swung in the darkness while the football game played on without them, her discomfort vanished completely. She sat in her bed filled with a renewed feeling of well-being.

She thought of Mr. Marchant and how he always had a nice smile and a pleasant word whenever he passed her in the hallway. She thought of how he usually had a twinkle in his eye while he was pretending to be gruff as he disciplined someone. She remembered seeing him on the front lawn, picking up candy bar wrappers, and in the hallway closing an occasional locker that some student had unthinkingly left open. She thought about the long hours he worked, and how sometimes on Saturdays his car would be the only car in the parking lot. *He must like being our principal,* Sara thought.

Sara decided to take the long way to school by way of a winding trail through the woods that came out onto the school grounds at the back side of the administration building.

Suddenly she heard a rustling in the bushes. Someone was coming, fast! She stopped and wheeled around, eager, and at the same time not eager, to discover what was rushing toward her. For a brief moment she felt like Little Red Riding Hood skipping through the forest; and she thought for a moment that something scary, like maybe the big bad wolf, might be romping through the bushes ready to eat her alive. And before she could laugh at her silly fantasy, Seth sprang from the bushes and into her full view.

"Seth!" she exclaimed gleefully. "Am I ever glad to see you! What happened to you yesterday? Why didn't you come to the tree house?"

"Because Mr. Marchant saw me cutting across the school yard. I had planned on blending in with the other students, but instead, I ran right into him. I was running across the front lawn when he came out of the administration building. It was only lucky that I didn't knock him right down."

Sara began to laugh. She couldn't stop laughing.

Seth laughed, too. He wasn't sure *why* he was

laughing, but he was enjoying Sara's laughing so much that he couldn't help but laugh right along with her.

Finally, Sara caught her breath and managed to get a few words out. "Seth, you're not going to believe this: Mr. Marchant saw me, too!"

"No. You're making that up." Seth laughed.

"No, really. I came around the building, and he looked right at me. I know he saw me."

"What did he say?"

"Nothing. He just looked at me, waved, and got in his car."

"*Oh, man!* Sara, can you believe it? What are the odds? What do you think is going to happen to us?"

"Well, they probably won't kill us," Sara said, trying to make light of the situation.

"*They* probably won't, but my parents will," Seth said.

Sara wanted to tell Seth everything that she had learned from Solomon about finding a better feeling place and about the *Law of Attraction*. But there was no time for all of that now.

They approached the school grounds, and as they came through a hedge row on the back side of the administration building, Sara dropped her book bag on the ground and sat on it while she took off a shoe and shook it, and a small rock tumbled out into the grass.

Seth stopped and waited for her. As he stood there in the shadow of the huge building, he could hear voices from the open window over their heads. "Shush," he whispered to Sara, holding his finger to his lips.

"*What?*" Sara whispered back.

As she stood up, she could hear Mr. Marchant and another teacher talking, then laughing.

"I think I just heard Mr. Marchant say my name. And your name!"

"*No way!*" Sara blurted.

"Shush. Listen."

Sara and Seth crouched down close to the building and listened as hard as they could. Sara's heart was pounding so hard she thought it would jump right into her mouth. She wasn't sure which was worse—that the principal of the school was talking about them, or that they were eavesdropping below his window.

"Well, what are you going to do about it?" Mr. Jorgensen asked.

"I've given it a lot of thought. In fact, most of last night I was thinking about it. And I've gotta tell you, my gut tells me to do nothing."

"I see."

Sara and Seth looked at each other. They could barely believe what they were hearing, or even that they were there beneath the window to hear it.

"You know, Chuck," Mr. Marchant continued,

114

"I've been thinking about kids today. Their lives are so different from when we were boys. They barely have an unscheduled moment to themselves. It seems to me that when we were kids— even though we had plenty of work to do—we had more time to ourselves. I remember lying out in the old apple orchard, seemed like for hours at a time, just watching the clouds floating by. And the biggest thing I had to worry about was not getting trampled by the horse eating apples from the tree over my head.

"I don't know where we got the time, and I don't remember anybody officially granting it to me, but *I* had time to think and daydream and plan. Time to explore and enjoy being a kid. And I just don't see that many kids today enjoying being kids. We've got 'em so damn scheduled. Seems like we've decided that they've got no common sense of their own, so we'd better make every decision for them. So we schedule their school time *and* their after-school time. I don't know how they stand it. I gotta tell you, Chuck, if I were a kid today, I think I'd go nuts. And I'd probably run away every now and again, *too.*"

"I know what you mean."

"These are good kids. I've known Sara all of her life. I've seen her go out of her way, over and over, to help out, or to make someone else feel better. And this new kid, Seth, that's his name, isn't it?

I'm hearing good things about him, too. These are special kids, Chuck. I'm not going to make an issue of this one. I don't think they'll make a habit of this. I mean, what's so terrible about wanting some time to be kids?"

The first bell rang, and Sara and Seth jumped so hard they bumped heads. They clamped their hands over their mouths to muffle the giggles that came next, and then they held their breaths, hoping to continue to be undetected.

"I'd appreciate it if you wouldn't mention this to anyone, Chuck. I don't want word getting out that I'm going soft or anything. And I don't want any precedents started here. Tomorrow I might think differently about all of this. It's just the way I'm gonna handle *this* one, ya know?"

"I do, Keith, and I agree with you. Hey, have a good day."

"Yeah, you, too."

Sara and Seth looked at each other in amazement. "I'll see you at the tree house," Seth whispered.

"Yeah," Sara whispered back. "See ya."

CHAPTER 18

A Forever Friendship

They had agreed to meet at the swinging tree every day after school, but for some reason Sara felt compelled to wait by the flagpole instead. *No one will notice if we walk together now and then. There are lots of kids who walk home together, or partway home,* Sara justified.

The big door banged closed, and Seth bounded down the front steps. He broke into a broad smile when he saw Sara waiting there.

"Sara, I'm glad you waited. I've got..."

"Hey, weirdo." Sara heard Len's mocking voice from behind them.

Sara wheeled around to see Len and Tommy, the two most obnoxious boys in town, no, in the whole world, standing behind them. They had never targeted *her* with their belittling remarks, but Sara had witnessed their hurtful teasing on many occasions, and with Solomon's help she had finally managed to pretty much tune them out. But she'd seen them bring many a classmate to tears, or close to it, with their rudeness. They weren't smart; they didn't get good grades; they didn't come from well-to-do families. Sara never understood how they had become so powerful.

"Sara, who's your new weird friend?" Tommy taunted.

"Hey, my name is Seth. Me, I've *always* been weird. At least for as long as I can remember. I got used to it a long time ago. Give it a while, *you'll* get used to it, too. Who are *you?*" Seth reached out quickly taking Tommy's hand and vigorously shaking it.

"Tom," Tom said flatly.

Seth shook his hand heartily; in fact, he shook it and shook it and shook it. Sara stifled a laugh. Seth had donned the attitude of some sort of weird comedic character as he continued to yank on Tommy's hand in a goofy, friendly gesture. Seth finally released Tommy's hand.

"And *your* name would be?" Seth questioned, now reaching for Len's hand.

Len jumped back as if Seth were a lion about to eat him. Holding both hands up and back as if someone had shouted, "Put 'em up!" he walked backward blubbering something like, "No, that's okay."

Len and Tommy ran off as if that lion were now chasing *them.*

Sara laughed and laughed.

"*What?*" Seth grinned.

"You are a genius, Seth Morris. I've never seen anything like that in my life."

"I don't know what you're talking about." Seth grinned.

"Yeah, *right!*" Sara laughed.

"Hey, Seth! *All right!*" someone yelled from a passing car.

Seth stopped smiling.

"What?" Sara asked. She didn't understand why Seth wasn't pleased with the praise he had attracted.

"Sara, I don't want to make enemies of those two, and I don't want anybody rallying behind me and using me as the front guy to fight their battles. But I've seen plenty of guys like those two. They feel so bad about themselves that the only way they can feel better is to put everyone else down. It doesn't work. It doesn't make them feel better, so they just get worse and worse. All I wanted to do is let them know that I'm not a good target for their fun. I wanted them to leave *me* alone. It's not my job to save the school from them. Everybody else can take care of themselves."

Sara was surprised to see Seth feeling so strongly about this. It was obvious that this wasn't a new experience for him and that he'd given all of this a great deal of thought. As Sara listened to Seth's logic, she couldn't help but notice that it was similar in some ways to things Solomon had told her. But Sara could see that he was still troubled about this.

Seth, Sara thought, *I've just got to tell you about Solomon!*

Sara remembered that Seth had begun to tell her something before Len and Tommy so rudely interrupted them. "Hey, what were you going to tell me?"

Sara could see Seth sifting back through his thoughts, reaching for whatever it was he seemed excited to tell her.

"Oh, nothin'. Nothin' that can't wait. Sara, I'd better go. I'll catch you tomorrow."

"Okay." Sara could tell that this wasn't a good time to push, but she was baffled. Seth seemed so happy when he came out of the building. He seemed strong and confident and in control, even jubilant as he dealt so perfectly with Len and Tommy, but his mood had abruptly changed as the kids shouted their approval from the passing cars. *Why had this bothered Seth so much?*

Seth had never told her about the miserable bus rides and obnoxious boys from his last school. He had pretty much put all of that out of his mind—until today, that is.

"Bummer," Sara said, under her breath, feeling sort of depressed that Seth wouldn't go to the swinging tree with her. She made her way there anyway and silently climbed the ladder up to the platform that Seth had built, and she stretched out on the bench using her book bag as a pillow.

"Solomon," Sara said out loud, "can you hear me? I need to talk with you about something."

No response from Solomon.

Sara remembered Solomon's words to her when he made his transition from her physical feathered friend to her nonphysical, nonfeathered friend: *Sara, our friendship is forever. And that means that anytime you would like a chat with Solomon, all you have to do is identify what you want to talk about and focus upon it, bring yourself to a place of feeling very good—and I'll be right here with you.*

She smiled as she thought about her dear feathered friend. She closed her eyes, basking in the warmth of the sunbeams filtering through the trees and warming her legs, and fell asleep.

CHAPTER 19

Dead . . . or Alive?

Sara opened her eyes, feeling very disoriented. "Well, *that's* a first," she said, out loud. "I don't usually nap in the tops of trees."

But I do. Sara heard a familiar clear voice coming from a branch up over her head.

Her heart began racing. "What in the world? Solomon, is that you? Is that *you?!*"

Hello, Sara, how are you today?

Tears began streaming down Sara's face as she peered through the leaves, spying a large, beautiful owl sitting out on the limb of her tree.

This is a very nice tree house, Sara. I can see why you spend so much time here.

"Solomon, Solomon, oh, Solomon! You've come back! You've come back!"

Sara, really, I don't know why you are so excited. I've never been gone.

"But Solomon, I can *see* you. You have feathers.

You *have* come back!"

Solomon smiled, quite pleased to see Sara so pleased.

Well, Sara, I thought it would be easier for Seth to experience me if he could see me as you did in the beginning. Besides, I wanted to spend time in your tree house.

Sara laughed. It was her dear, sweet, funny Solomon, all right. Sara felt happier than she could ever remember feeling. "Oh, Solomon, I'm *so* happy you are back!"

It's hard to get over the dead or alive thing, isn't it, Sara? Remember, you are not dead or alive. You are always alive. What is it about my feathers that's so important to you mortals anyway?

Sara laughed. She did understand what Solomon had taught her—that there is no death and all Beings live forever. But there was no getting around it. Sara loved being able to see Solomon as she heard him. She loved peering into his wonderful, wise eyes and gazing at his beautiful feathers softly moving in the breeze. She loved watching him spread his amazing big wings and lift, powerfully, up into the sky.

Sara, we are going to have a wonderful time as we help Seth remember who he is. He is pondering many important things, and it is for that reason, in response to his asking, that I have returned.

Sara smiled. She felt such joy and such love, and such an excited feeling of eagerness.

Sara, I'm going to leave it to you to introduce us.

"But Solomon, what should I say?"

Use your own judgment. I'm sure you will think of the right thing to say. Tell Seth about me tomorrow, and when the time is right, I'll join you.

Have a wonderful evening, sweet Sara. I'll see you later.

"Solomon, I am so glad to see you again."

Well, Sara, it's nice to be seen.

Sara laughed.

Solomon lifted from the branch, made one very large circle in the sky, and then flew out of Sara's view.

"Yippee!" Sara's voice echoed through the trees. She ran and skipped all the way home.

CHAPTER 20

No Turning Back

Oh, darn, it's raining! Sara could hardly believe it. It almost never rained in Sara's town. During the winter there was lots of snow, and then during the spring and summer the snow slowly melted, providing all the water that Sara's community, and many other communities downstream, needed. Rain was rare.

Of all the days for it to rain. This was the day Sara had planned to tell Seth about Solomon. *But we can't go to the tree house in the rain,* Sara silently complained.

The final bell rang and Sara waited inside the building. She laughed as she looked out into the school yard watching students running here and there like chickens with their heads cut off. No one had an umbrella. Some were holding jackets over their heads, some tried to shield themselves with books, and all of them looked disoriented and awkward. *Good grief,* Sara thought, *it's only a little water. It's not like they're going to melt or anything.*

"Hey, Sara," Seth called, as he ran down the steps toward her, "I'm glad you waited. I was afraid you'd go on home on account of the rain."

"Yeah, bummer. Guess we can't swing from the tree today." Sara hadn't planned on doing much swinging, anyway. What she really wanted was to sit and talk with Seth.

"We probably shouldn't swing today, but we can go to the tree house anyway. I put a tarp up this morning on my way to school. It should be fairly dry under that. Mom says I can hang out an extra half hour. Since it's wet out I don't have so much to do. Wanna go?"

"All right!" Sara was grinning from ear to ear. Not only was this unusual rain not a problem—it was turning out to be a help.

"Hey, what made you think of the tarp? It wasn't raining this morning."

"My mom said it would rain before the day was out. She says she can feel it in her elbow. She never misses. It's a gift."

"You have a very weird mother," Sara said, laughing.

"Takes one to know one!" Seth laughed back.

Sara laughed. *Well, he's about to find out just exactly how weird I am.*

But for some strange reason Sara wasn't really worried about this. In fact, it seemed to her that a whole series of rather odd circumstances had perfectly set the stage for her long-overdue chat with Seth. She could feel that the timing for this was just right. The whole thing seemed to have a sense of inevitability about it. It was as if it were all in motion and there was no turning back—and no desire to turn back.

This feeling reminded Sara of sitting on a gunnysack sled at the top of the giant slippery slide on her first visit to the amusement park. She remembered how hesitant she had felt, how unready she really was, but then her brother, Jason, shoved her from behind, and an instant later she was barreling down the slide. She knew that there was no turning back, and in the fun of the ride down the slide, she no longer wanted to.

All of this felt just like that. And Sara knew that she was about to begin her joyful ride down the slide.

CHAPTER 21

A Teaching Owl

Sara and Seth sat high in their tree. "Do you think your parents know about this place?" Sara asked Seth.

"I'm not sure. But I can't believe that they know, 'cause if they did know, they'd probably be figuring out things that needed to be done to keep me from spending so much time here. And yet, I can't believe that they haven't figured out that I'm going *somewhere* after school."

Sara sat back against the tree and pulled her legs up close against her chest and then pulled her jacket down over her legs. She was always fascinated by the stories Seth told of his life at home. It was hard for Sara to imagine having parents who were so strict. It wasn't that Sara didn't have responsibilities. She had plenty of them. But it always felt to Sara that it was important to her parents that she have a good life and a good time. She never felt that they were trying to come between her and a happy life. They didn't stand on their heads to make Sara's life perfect—nothing like that, but they didn't get in the way of it either.

It seemed to Sara that Seth's parents deliberately made his life hard. As if a hard life would somehow make him turn out better or stronger or something.

"We just have to have as much fun as we can *while* we can, Sara," Seth said.

Well, I guess this is as good a time as any, Sara thought. *Here goes.* She gulped. She just couldn't seem to find the words to begin.

Solomon was aware of Sara's struggle.

Sara, Solomon spoke in Sara's mind, *are you worried about Seth disapproving of you?*

"Maybe," Sara said out loud.

"Maybe *what?*" Seth asked.

Sara was concentrating so hard on what Solomon might say that she didn't even realize Seth had spoken to her.

Sara, rather than worrying about whether Seth will approve of you, think, instead, of the value you are giving to him.

Sara's fear vanished. A flood of wonderful memories washed over Sara as she realized, in that moment, the extraordinary value *she* had discovered in knowing Solomon.

"Of course," Sara said, out loud.

"Of course, *what?*" Seth said. "Sara, you're beginning to *scare* me."

Sara brought her attention back to the tree house and to her friend sitting before her.

"Well, Seth, are you ready for the next chapter of my strange but wonderful life?"

Seth smiled. He'd been dying to hear more about her owl experience, but he'd decided to wait for it to be *her* idea. "You bet!"

"Okay, here goes," Sara said.

"Remember, I told you about how I fell on the ice and how I heard a voice that said, *Have you forgotten that you cannot drown?*"

"I remember."

"And how I saw this amazing, gigantic owl?"

Seth nodded eagerly.

"Well, the next day I went back to the thicket to see if I could find him again. And when I walked into the thicket, there he was, sitting right there on a fence post, right in front of my face."

"I've seen lots of owls," Seth said, "but not up close like that. Were you scared?"

Sara took a big breath. "No, I didn't feel scared because it was all happening so fast. He said to me, *Hello, Sara, isn't this a lovely day?*"

Sara spoke slowly, studying Seth's face for some sort of reaction, but Seth was quiet. That was even worse. She almost wished he would laugh, and then she could just pretend she was making it all up to tease him, and then they could swing from the rope and just forget it.

"Go on," Seth said slowly.

"Well, I mean, his mouth wasn't moving, or anything like that, but I could hear what he was thinking. He knew my name, and he said he had been waiting for me. He said that he was a teacher and that I was a teacher, too. He knows every-thing, Seth. He's funny and smart and will talk about whatever I want to talk about. He says that all is well, and that whatever happens in our lives is because we're making it happen."

Sara's mouth was so dry she almost felt panic. She was in too deep to back out now, but she felt too paralyzed to go any further with her story. She had never told any of this to anyone.

"Sara, I don't believe this! This is too weird!"

"I shouldn't have told you!"

"No, Sara. I believe you. I believe you. I meant that it's weird because a bird talked to me once, too. At least, I think he did. It only happened once, and then later I thought maybe I had dreamed it or hallucinated it or something. I never told *anyone* about it. They would have locked me up!"

Sara felt such relief. "Really! A bird talked to *you?*"

"It was a red cardinal. I was hunting one day for something for dinner. We used to pretty much eat anything we could shoot or catch . . ."

"Hmm," Sara murmured. His life was so very different from hers.

"...and one day I was sitting out in the pasture on a stump, just waiting for something to show up, and this big red cardinal landed on the fence real close to me. So I got it in my gun sight and right while it was looking at me, I shot it.

"It just dropped off the fence and landed in the snow. It was so red, just layin' there in that white snow.

"I went up to see it and I thought, *Geez, why did I do that? It's too little to eat.* I felt real bad. It seemed like such a terrible waste."

A tear rolled down Seth's cheek.

"And then the bird spoke to me. He even knew my name."

"What did he say?"

"He said, *Seth, there is no need to feel bad. For there is no waste, and there is no death. All is well here. All is well.* But just the same, that was the last thing I ever shot."

"Wow!" Sara's eyes filled with tears, too. "That sounds just like something Solomon would say."

Seth wiped his face with his sleeve; Sara did the same, and they sat huddled in their tree house overwhelmed with emotion. Neither spoke.

Solomon circled above their tree house, waiting to make his perfect entrance.

There'll never be a better time than this, Solomon said, as he plunged straight down from the sky as if he intended to dive right into the river. But then he pulled up quickly, just at the last minute, and zoomed back up to the tree house and landed on a branch only a few feet from Seth and Sara.

"Geez, Louise!" Seth shouted, jumping to his feet.

Louise is a nice name. Solomon smiled. *However, Sara calls me Solomon.*

Seth flopped down on the bench, as if his legs just couldn't hold him, and looked in amazement at Sara.

Sara grinned and shrugged. "What can I say?"

Sara went to bed that night feeling a contentment beyond anything she had ever felt before. The thrill of having her Solomon back in physical form, where she could see him and touch him, was almost more wonderful than she could bear. And on top of that, to have her two very best friends in the whole world now knowing each other, well, there just couldn't be anything greater than that. And it was obvious to Sara that their appreciation of each other was mutual.

Sara snuggled deep down into her bed and pulled the blankets right up over her head. She felt so very, very happy.

CHAPTER 22

Let's Fly Together

Sara awakened in the middle of the night. Her room was very dark and she lay there for a moment wondering why she was awake. Then, off in the far corner of the room, up near the ceiling, she noticed a soft white light. "What in the world?!" Sara exclaimed, sitting up in her bed and rubbing her eyes to try to get them to focus better.

The glow became brighter, and when Sara opened her eyes, she could clearly see the essence of Solomon. It was like seeing the ghost version of her fine feathered friend.

"Solomon?" Sara questioned. "Is that *you?*"

Good evening, Sara. I hope you don't mind that I wakened you. I wondered if you might like to come and fly with us.

"Yes, of course. You bet, I'm ready . . . with *us? Who's us?*"

Seth is in the tree house tonight. He's swinging from the tree. He is so happy; he just couldn't sleep. I thought it might be a good time for a night flight. What do you think?

Sara's heart felt so happy she thought she might burst. She had never forgotten the night flights Solomon had escorted her on, but it had been quite a while since the last one. Nothing in her experience either before or since had even come close to the wonder and beauty of those flights. And now Solomon was inviting her again, and best of all, her friend Seth would be coming along, too.

Get dressed and go to the tree house, Sara. Seth will be glad to see you. I'll meet you there.

"Great, Solomon. I'll see you there."

Solomon disappeared.

Sara slipped out of bed and quietly dressed. She remembered flying with Solomon before and how perfectly comfortable she had been, flying in her nightgown, even though that flight had been in the middle of the winter. She wasn't sure why she was bundling up so much, but it seemed like the right thing to do since she was certain it must be below 40 degrees outside. She quietly slipped out the back door, crossed the backyard, and left for Thacker's Trail.

There was no moon visible, and it was very dark. But as she walked, Sara's eyes adjusted to the darkness, and she easily made her way along this familiar trail, feeling her way, or sensing her way, through the trees. She smiled as she noticed that even though she was out in the middle of the night, all alone, she felt not even one little bit of fear.

She heard a sort of "whoosh" in the trees. She stopped and listened hard to see if she could hear it again. Then *whoosh . . . whoosh . . . whoosh . . .* and a thud. Sara smiled.

Just as Solomon had said, Seth was swinging from the tree. Sara stood still, back in the shadows. How could she let him know that she was there without startling him?

She cupped her hands over her mouth and called, "Whoo, whoo, whoo . . ." in as owl-like a fashion as she could.

Seth heard the owl sound and stood frozen in his tracks.

"Whoo, whoo, whoo . . ." Sara called again.

"Solomon, is that *you?*" she heard Seth ask.

Sara grinned.

Seth cupped his hands and called back, "Whoo, whoo, whoo . . ."

"Whoo, whoo, whoo . . ." Sara replied.

"Whoo, whoo, whoo . . ." Seth answered back.

"Whoo are you?" Sara cooed, then giggled.

Seth recognized Sara's voice. "Sara, what in the world are *you* doing out here!"

"I might ask you the same thing." Sara laughed. "Sorry about the owl call, but I didn't want to startle you."

"I just couldn't sleep, Sara. This Solomon thing is so cool. I can hardly believe that it's really happening; I kept wondering if I dreamed it."

"I know. When *I* first met Solomon, I woke up the next morning thinking I had dreamed it, or that maybe *I* was crazy. And I never did tell anyone else, either, because I was sure they'd think I was crazy. But it's *not* crazy, Seth. It's wonderful, and it is *real*."

"I know. It's neat, Sara, but it *is* sorta weird. I'm glad we can talk about it together."

"I have an idea that it's about to get weirder."

"What do you mean, Sara?"

"Well, Solomon woke me up about an hour ago and said that you were in the tree house and that if I'd meet you here, the three of us could fly together."

From over their heads, Seth and Sara heard: *Whoo, whoo, whoo. . . .* Sara laughed. She knew it was Solomon. However, in all the time that Sara had known Solomon, this was the first time, ever, he had said, *Whoo, whoo, whoo. . . .*

"Hi, Solomon," Sara said. She knew Solomon was talking owl-talk to tease them.

Good evening, my little owl friends. Are you ready to come fly with me? Solomon flew down to a limb just over their heads.

"Really, Solomon?" Seth exclaimed. "We can fly with you? Oh, man, I can't believe this!"

Seth, you've flown before, haven't you? It seems to me that I can recall many flights out in the countryside overlooking your farms.

"Oh, you mean dream flying. Oh yeah, I used to do that all the time. In fact, just about every night, I'd fly in my dreams. But then the dreams stopped. I'm not sure why, but I think it was on account of something Mrs. Gilliland said."

"What did she say?" Sara asked.

"She said that flying dreams were wrong."

"Whatever could be wrong with a flying dream?" Sara exclaimed. "They're just about the best kind of dream a person could have."

"She said flying dreams are about sex," Seth blurted out and then blushed. He could hardly believe he had said such a thing in front of Sara.

Sara blushed, too.

"The next night I was flying, pretty much like usual, out over the farm and the lake and around, and then I flew into a cave. As I flew in, it got narrower and narrower, and I just kept flying deeper and deeper into the cave until I got wedged deep in a crack—and there I was, stuck in that crack."

"Then what happened?" Sara asked.

"I woke up—and that was the very last flying dream I ever had."

Sara was wide-eyed.

Solomon smiled. *Well, Seth, I think it's time for you to free yourself from the bondage of that cave, and from the bondage of what other people think. It's time for you to fly again.*

"I'm ready. What do I have to do?"

Sara, why don't you explain it to Seth.

"Well," Sara hesitated, trying to remember back to *her* first flying instructions, "first you have to really *want* to fly."

"Oh, I do!" Seth said.

"And then," Sara continued, "you have to find the feeling-place of flying."

"What do you mean, *find the feeling-place?*"

"Well, like, you have to remember what it *feels* like to fly, or think about how much fun it is to fly."

"That's easy," Seth said. And in that instant, Seth and Sara felt a whoosh within them that took their breaths away—and up, up, up, up, up into the top of the tree they arose.

Sara and Seth both laughed as they rose higher and higher and then floated right up out of the top of the tree.

"I thought swinging from the tree was great! Sara, this is *amazing!*"

Sara beamed. As much as she loved flying with Solomon, watching Seth flying for the first time was even better.

Sara, I'll leave you to show Seth around town tonight. Have fun. We'll talk more tomorrow.

Solomon flew off into the distance.

"Where to?" Seth said, with an excitement in his voice Sara had never heard before.

"You may go wherever you want to go." Sara remembered Solomon's words to her, way back on *her* first flight.

"Let's go to the cave," Seth said, heading off in that direction.

Sara followed along behind. She laughed. "Is this sort of like getting back on the horse after you've fallen off?" (She thought it was funny that Seth was willing to go right back into a cave when his last flying dream had ended so terribly, stuck in a crack in a cave.)

"Yeah, something like that," Seth called back.

They soared across the night sky, swooping down close to the river to rapidly make their way out to the cave.

"This sure beats wading up the river."

"Sure does," Sara answered.

Seth dived down into the entrance to the cave.

Sara followed him.

Neither felt any fear.

"Hello, hello!"

"Hello, hello!" the cave echoed back.

They slowly glided deep into the cave, where

the narrow tunnel broke out into a very large room. And then they stopped and floated, looking down into this vast space.

On the walls and ceilings of the cave were painted pictures of animals.

"I wonder how they got up here so high to paint these pictures?"

"You mean up here where *we* are?" Sara laughed. "Maybe we aren't the first ones to fly in this cave."

Sara and Seth slowly flew deep into the cave. "Seth, this cave is enormous! It must go back in here for miles!"

They flew down another long corridor, which broke out again into another large room. Then down another corridor and another and another. Sara followed along behind Seth, feeling amazement that something so extraordinary could have been right there in the mountain above her town all of her life, without her knowing about it.

Deeper and deeper they flew. *I hope you know what you're doing, Seth!* Sara thought, remembering Seth's awful dream and feeling a bit claustrophobic as she noticed that the tunnel was getting smaller and smaller.

As they turned the next corner, Sara caught her breath. Looking straight ahead, the tunnel seemed to come to an abrupt end. But Seth continued to fly straight into the cave. Sara opened her mouth to scream because it looked like he was about to plunge head-on into a giant stone wall when Seth suddenly disappeared from Sara's view. The tunnel had turned upward, and Seth had zoomed right up out into the moonlight. Sara zoomed up out of the cave, right behind Seth.

Seth's joyful *Yippees!* were echoing across the valley.

Well, I guess Seth's been liberated from his cave dream, Sara thought.

"Hey, Sara, look, the moon's out!" Seth called, as he zoomed back down across the valley.

"Sara, I want to fly forever and ever!"

Sara remembered speaking those exact words on *her* first glorious flight.

"But I guess we should be getting back before somebody misses us. It's almost sunup."

"I'll race you to the tree house," Sara called, as she streaked across the sky.

"No fair," Seth called out, doing his best to catch up.

When Seth caught up with Sara, she was floating up over the tree, high above the tree house. Seth flew to her side and they giggled as they floated there together.

"Okay, Seth, let me show you this neat way to get down. Just point one foot down, and *down* you'll go."

Sara and Seth held hands and pointed one

foot downward, and down, down, down into their tree house they dropped.

"Wow!" Seth said.

"I know," Sara replied.

"If I never have another neat experience for as long as I live, *this* one will have been enough!"

"I used to say that," Sara laughed, "but I keep finding out that as good as it gets, I still want more. Solomon said that's normal, and that it's not greedy, either. Solomon says that *we're supposed to have spectacular lives.*"

"Sounds good to me, Sara. Do you want me to walk you home?" Seth asked.

"Nah, I'm okay. See ya tomorrow."

"Yeah, Sara, See ya. And thanks."

CHAPTER 23
The Law of Attraction

Sara and Seth sat perched in the tree house, high in their tree, overlooking the river below. Sunlight filtered down through the leaves, making moving patterns on the platform where they were sitting. Sara scooted over a bit to catch more sunbeams on her body; she loved the feeling of being just a little bit too chilly and then finding a warm sunbeam to bask in.

Seth watched her making herself perfectly comfortable. He couldn't help but notice how at ease she seemed. He, on the other hand, wasn't feeling at ease at all. He squirmed about, first on the bench, then sitting down on the platform and leaning back against the bench. *I don't know what I'm so nervous about,* he thought.

Solomon sat on the branch just over their heads, waiting for them to get situated. Solomon smiled as he observed Sara, his longtime student, relaxed and basking, although still eager for her chat with Solomon that was about to take place, while Seth, his very new student, seemed to be struggling with anxiety.

This too shall pass, Solomon thought, and as that thought showered like the filtered sunlight down over Solomon's waiting students, Seth took a deep breath, leaned back, and relaxed.

Well, my fine featherless friends, what would you like to talk about today? Solomon began.

Both Sara and Seth laughed.

It is, indeed, a beautiful day, Solomon added.

"Sure is," Seth said.

Sara smiled. She knew that Seth was in for such a wonderful treat. She loved her chats with Solomon and just knew that Seth would feel the same way. Sara had discovered early on in her experience with Solomon that her wise friend had very little to say unless she had something that she wanted to talk about. She had also discovered that it was never difficult to think of something to discuss. Her life experience at school and at home always seemed to provide situations that needed some clarification; and she had come to know that whatever she wanted clarification about, or hard answers for, Solomon was always ready, willing, and able to assist.

Sara recalled that in the beginning, there were so many things that she didn't understand—many things that seemed unfair or unjust or just down-right wrong. But over time, while chatting with Solomon over situation after situation, Sara had come to understand the basis of Solomon's philoso-phy—and, in time, she had come to be able to sort out her own answers to many of the questions that would arise in her daily life.

The most significant thing that Sara had noticed—that had occurred in her life since meet-ing her friend Solomon—was that she had a con-tinuing sense of well-being. Solomon had helped Sara understand that no matter how things *seem* to appear in any moment in time, the truth is that all really *is* well. And while Sara struggled with that understanding at times, even arguing with Solo-mon on occasion, she had come to mostly know that this was true.

Solomon sat waiting. Seth wasn't sure what was supposed to happen. Sara began.

"So, Seth, you can ask Solomon anything you want. He has answers to *everything.*"

Seth shifted his position.

"Do you have something important that you have been wondering about?" Sara continued.

Seth folded his legs in front of him and leaned forward, twiddling his thumbs. He looked deep in thought.

"Well, yeah, I mean, I've wondered about lots

of things. I've got questions saved up since I was four years old."

Seth's mind was spinning, and he found it difficult to focus. He could hardly believe that anyone, even this amazing owl who had taught him to fly, would hold the answers to all of the questions he had.

Well, Seth, Solomon began quietly, *the good news is, you don't have to ask them all at once. And the other good news is that there is no limit to the answers that will come to you. No quantity limit and no time limit. You may take as long as you like, continuing to ask questions.*

"What's the *bad* news?" Seth asked.

Oh, that? There is no bad news, Seth. Solomon smiled.

Sara leaned back against the tree and grinned. She liked this already.

Seth was beginning to focus, and things he had been wondering about began to flood into his mind. "Okay, Solomon, I've got some questions: How come life is so unfair? I mean, how come some people have such good lives and some people have such bad ones? . . . Why are people allowed to be mean to each other? . . . And why do bad things happen? . . . How come people have to die or get sick, and why do we have to kill and eat animals? . . . Why do floods wash away some people's farms while other people are starving because the lack

148

of rain doesn't allow their food to grow? . . . Why do most people have to work so hard every day of their lives and then die, tired, with nothin' to show for all of their hard work? . . . And why do countries fight with each other? Why can't they just leave each other alone? Why do . . . ?"

Sara sat wide-eyed. She had never seen anyone fire off so many questions in such a short period of time in her life. *Seth has asked more questions in the first five minutes than I did in the first five months,* she thought.

Seth was continuing. "What happened to all of the Indians who used to live here, and what gave the white man the right to take their land and destroy their lives, and . . . ?"

Sara looked at Solomon. She wondered if Solomon had ever heard so many questions all at the same time before, either.

Solomon listened patiently.

Finally, Seth stopped. He looked up at Solomon and leaned back against the tree. He was breathing heavily. Almost panting.

Solomon began. *Well, Seth, we have a saying around here: "Ask, and it is given." I cannot remember visiting with anyone who had more questions than you. And it is my promise to you that for each of your questions, you will receive an answer. It is also my promise that with each of those answers, you will have more questions. In the beginning, sometimes the answers will not satisfy you completely. It takes a little while for them to sink in. But in time, you will fully understand everything you want to understand. We will have a glorious time together. That is certain.*

Sara was surprised at the tone of Seth's questions. *He seems so angry. He's so focused on what's unfair,* Sara thought.

Solomon looked at Sara. *Seth's questions remind me of your first questions, Sara.*

Sara was caught by surprise. Seth and Solomon were talking with each other, and Sara nearly forgot that Solomon always knew what was on her mind. She tried to remember *her* first questions to Solomon. It seemed like such a long time ago.

Remember Donald? Sara heard Solomon's voice in her head.

Sara grinned. *Oh, yeah, I do remember him.*

Sara sat back and recalled how indignant she had felt when the school bullies were picking on Donald, the new student in town. Those high-running emotions that were so real back then felt so distant to her now. She leaned back against the tree again, realizing just how far she'd come.

Sara looked at Seth earnestly plying Solomon with questions, and she loved it. She marveled that while Solomon was conversing with Seth— catching every piece of what Seth was asking—he was, at the same time, holding a discussion with her in *her* mind. She felt a joyous bubble burst in her chest in seeming response to this discovery. She shivered with excitement as she realized that her Solomon experience was expanding into new levels.

It is always satisfying for a born teacher to watch another teacher at work, Sara. She heard Solomon's voice in her head. *We will have a glorious unfolding here.*

Sara smiled. She could hardly wait.

She focused her attention on what Solomon and Seth were talking about. Seth was quiet now, and Solomon had begun.

Seth, these are wonderful questions. I can see that you've given a great deal of thought to these things. Now, let's see, where to begin?

Sara, Seth, and Solomon were silent. It seemed especially quiet after the barrage of questions Seth had hurled at Solomon. Solomon didn't begin speaking right away. It seemed to Sara that he was somehow calculating everything that Seth had asked, and was now sorting it out to begin his answers in an orderly unfolding.

Solomon spoke. *Here is the beginning point. This is the first thing you must come to understand before any other answers will make sense: There is no injustice.*

Sara's eyes flashed from Solomon to Seth. Both were momentarily quiet. Sara felt uneasy; she knew that answer wasn't going to sit well with Seth. It seemed to her that every question he had asked was about injustice. And in one short sentence, Solomon seemed to be discounting the basis of all that Seth wanted to know.

Seth looked tense, but before he could gather his thoughts and begin to protest, Solomon continued.

Seth, before we begin to discuss the specific issues you have raised, I want to give you an understanding of how this magnificent Universe works. And once you understand these basics and have an opportunity to observe them in your own life, then it will be easier for you to understand how they consistently affect not only your life but everyone else's as well.

Seth sat up straighter and stared intently at Solomon. Sara smiled. She could hardly wait to hear Solomon begin to explain the *Law of Attraction* to Seth.

Are there laws in this town that affect the people who live here?

"Sure. Probably lots of them," Seth responded.

Name one.

"Speed-limit laws. You can only drive 35 miles per hour on Main Street," Seth replied.

Which do you think is the most powerful law, Seth, the law of 35 miles per hour or the law of gravity?

Seth grinned. "That's easy, Solomon. Gravity must be way more important than a speed law."

Why is that?

"Because," Seth continued, enthusiastically, "only *some* people are affected by the 35-mile-per-hour law, but *everyone* is affected by the law of gravity."

Solomon smiled. *Very good. The 35-mile-per-hour law can easily be ignored. It's not so easy to ignore the law of gravity.*

"Right." Seth laughed.

There is another much more powerful law. Much greater than the law of gravity. It is the <u>Law of Attraction.</u> And just as your law of gravity affects everything that exists upon your planet, the <u>Law of Attraction</u> affects everything that exists in all of the Universe, in all space and in all time, and in all that is spaceless and timeless. In fact, this <u>Law of Attraction</u> is actually the basis of everything that exists.

Solomon had Seth's attention. Seth leaned forward waiting for more.

The <u>Law of Attraction,</u> in simple terms, says, "That which is like unto itself, is drawn." In more complicated terms, it means that everything in the Universe is emitting a vibrational signal—and those signals that are the same come together, magnetically.

Sara watched Seth's face carefully. She remembered how difficult it had been for *her* to grasp these new ideas at first, and she wondered how Seth was doing with it.

"You mean, like radio signals?" Seth asked.

Very much like that, Solomon answered.

Sara smiled.

You see, Seth, the entire Universe is vibrationally

based. Everything is vibrating. And it is through these vibrations that things either come together or stay apart. "That which is like unto itself is drawn."

"Well, how do you know which things have the same signals?"

You can look around and see the things that are together. That's one way. And with some practice, you can begin to read the vibrational signal of things even before they do actually come together. You can actually read the signal prior to the physical manifestation.

"Hmm," Seth pondered. "Neat."

Sara smiled again. This was going very well.

"Do *I* offer a signal?"

Indeed, you do.

"Does *everyone?*"

Yes, indeed.

"Well, then, how do I know what signal *I'm* offering?"

You can tell by the way you feel, and by what kinds of things are coming to you.

"Can I tell what signal *others* are offering?"

It isn't your work to keep track of that, but you can tell what they are offering by what is coming to them, and by the way they seem to feel. Their attitudes and moods tell you a great deal about how they are doing.

"So, how can I match up with signals like mine?"

That's not your work, either. The <u>Law of Attraction</u> will do the matching up.

"Is it possible to offer a signal on purpose?"

Yes, indeed, it is possible to offer your signal on purpose—and that is what I have come to teach you.

"Whew!" Sara squealed, right out loud. She felt so much exhilaration that she thought she was going to fly right up out of the tree. She was so impressed with how clear Seth's mind was, and she loved the power of his questions and how easily he seemed to grasp Solomon's answers.

We'll talk more tomorrow, Solomon said.

"Oh, man," Seth complained, not wanting this to end so soon. "I've got, like, a million more questions, Solomon. Do we have to stop now?"

Seth, we'll talk more about everything you've asked. For the first few days every answer will foster within you dozens of new questions. But before you know it, you'll have a basis of understanding, and then everything you want to know will fall easily into place.

I have enjoyed this interaction immensely.

"Me, too, Solomon," Sara and Seth chimed together as if they were one voice.

Hmm, there you have it. Two Beings in perfect vibrational harmony.

Sara and Seth looked at each other while Solomon lifted up and out of the tree and disappeared.

"Pretty cool, huh?" Sara asked.

"Ya got that right," Seth replied.

CHAPTER 24

Attention to Vibrations

Seth and Sara met in the tree house and waited for Solomon.

"I wonder where he is," Sara said.

The wind suddenly gusted and leaves fluttered down from the tree. Sara blinked and rubbed her eyes as dust flew in; Seth spit out the dirt and a piece of a leaf that had flown into his mouth—and in the middle of all of this commotion, Solomon dropped right down onto the platform.

Seth and Sara jumped in surprise.

Sorry about that, Solomon said. *I was trying a new landing. It needs work.*

Sara didn't know what to make of that. She had never seen Solomon do anything like that in all of the time she'd known him.

"You mean, *you're* still learning things, too?" Seth asked, in amazement.

Of course. We are all continually becoming more.

"But I thought you knew everything!" Seth and Sara said again at the same time.

Solomon smiled. *What would be the fun in that? Now, that would be a very sad state of affairs, to have discovered all that there is to discover, to truly be finished, finally, once and for all. I assure you there is none of that. There is no such thing as finished. There is only eternal, everlasting, joyous motion forward.*

Solomon settled onto the platform and, using his beak, straightened some feathers into place. *There, that's much better,* he said. *Now, let's see. Where should we begin?*

"Well," Seth began, "last night I kept thinking about what you said about offering my own signal. I don't know why, but that kept coming into my head over and over again. I don't even really understand what it means, but I kept thinking about it anyway."

Solomon smiled. *I am very pleased that of all the things we talked about, that is what stuck in your mind the most—because that is the most important thing that I have to teach you.*

Sara leaned forward with interest. Solomon was saying much of the same things that she had learned, but with Seth he seemed to be using different words. She wanted to be sure that she understood this thing that Solomon said was the most important thing.

First, you must understand how it is that you offer

a signal: Your signal has to do with what you are perceiving.

"Perceiving?"

Yes, what you are giving your attention to, what you are focusing on. For example, when you are remembering, you are offering your vibrational signal. When you are observing or looking or thinking about something, you are offering your signal. When you are pondering or studying or examining or imagining, you are offering your signal.

"What about when I'm talking about something?"

Especially then, because when you are speaking of something, it usually has your full attention.

"Gee, Solomon, it seems like we're offering our signal in just about everything we're doing."

Good, Seth. That is exactly right. And since the Universe is constantly matching your signal with things that are like your signal, it is very good when you are offering your signal on purpose.

"Well, that makes sense, Solomon. But what happens when I see something that's terrible? Something that's bad or wrong? What happens to my signal then?"

Your signal is always affected by whatever you are giving your attention to.

Sara watched Seth. She could feel his discomfort. She remembered how hard it had been for her to understand this part at first.

"But Solomon," Seth protested, "how can I ever help anything get better if I don't give my attention to what is wrong with it to begin with?"

It is certainly appropriate to give your attention to it—to begin with. In fact, that is the way you decide how you can help or what it is that would be better, or what it is that you do want. The important thing is to decide, as quickly as you can, what would be better or what is wanted—and then give your full attention to that. Then the Universe can go to work on matching that.

"Oh, I see," Seth said hesitantly.

With a bit of practice, you will always be able to tell what your vibrational signal is. You will come to know that the way you feel is a very good indicator of your signal: The better you feel, the better. The worse you feel, the worse. It's really not very complicated.

"Hmm . . ." Seth was quiet. Sara wasn't sure if that was because he understood, or because he didn't believe Solomon. He had seemed more interested when Solomon was talking about radio signals and vibrations, but when Solomon began talking about feelings and emotions, Seth seemed to close down.

You see, Solomon continued, *most human Beings are dealing with vibrations all of the time; they just don't know that they are. Everything about your physical world has a vibrational basis. The reason your eyes see what they see is because your eyes understand*

159

*vibration. What you hear is because your ears under-
stand vibration. Even what you smell and taste and
feel with your fingers is because your body is understanding vibration.*

Seth brightened. "I remember when one of
my teachers brought tuning forks to school. Every
fork was a different size. She had a little hammer
that she would hit them with, and she told us that
the reason why they sounded different was because
they had different vibrations."

*Very good, Seth. And in that same way, everything
in the Universe is offering different vibrations—and you
are observing those different vibrations with your physical senses: your nose, your eyes, your ears, your fingertips,
the taste buds on your tongue. In fact, everything you
perceive or see or understand around you is your interpre-
tation of vibration.*

Solomon was using many words that Seth, and
Sara, too, for that matter, weren't really sure of.
But the more Solomon spoke, the more they were
understanding.

"Are you saying that a flower is offering a
vibration, my nose is receiving that vibration, and
that's why I can smell the flower?"

*That is exactly right, Seth. Have you noticed that
different flowers have different fragrances?*

"Yes. And some don't have any fragrance at
all."

Have you ever smelled a flower that somebody else couldn't smell?

"My mother smells flowers that I can't smell. I always thought she was just pretending."

Solomon smiled. *Everyone does not smell the same scents, just as everyone does not see the same. Have you ever noticed that dogs are able to smell things that you cannot?*

"Dogs smell things that I wouldn't *want* to smell!" Seth said, laughing as he spoke.

Sara laughed, too.

Solomon smiled. *Have you noticed that dogs can hear things that you can't hear?*

"Yeah, I have," Seth said.

So, Solomon continued, *not only are all kinds of things offering all kinds of different vibrations, but different receivers are receiving differently.*

Play with this for a few days. See what kinds of things you observe that teach you about vibrations, and then we'll talk again. I have enjoyed this interaction immensely.

And before Sara and Seth could protest, Solomon was up and away.

"He sure doesn't dawdle when he's ready to go, does he?" Seth laughed.

"That's true." Sara smiled.

"Okay, Sara, I'll see you here tomorrow after school. We'll compare notes about what we've observed."

"Okay. See ya."

Sara was so pleased that Seth was excited about what he was learning from Solomon that she was almost home before she realized they hadn't even bothered to swing from the tree. "Hmm."

CHAPTER 25

A Fun Day

When Sara walked onto the school grounds, she noticed something shining very brightly from one of the windows on the ground floor.

"What in the world?" Sara mumbled, as she continued to gaze in the direction of this strange new light.

As she walked toward it, she concluded that it was coming from Miss Ralph's art room. It was a very weird thing. One minute it looked red, then blue, then green . . . Sara just couldn't take her eyes off it.

Although Sara had helped her carry art materials to her car, she had never actually been inside of Miss Ralph's classroom, but she was going in today. She had to find out what was causing this amazing light show in her window.

The classroom door was still closed and when Sara pulled on the knob, the door banged open.

She didn't realize how excited she had been or how hard she was pulling on the door until it banged back against the wall. The pretty teacher jumped away from the window, startled at the loud noise.

"Can I help you?"

Sara was embarrassed that she had made such a racket. "I saw something shining from your window. You can see it clear across the parking lot. I wondered what it is?"

Miss Ralph smiled and touched the prism with her finger, causing it to spin on its string and cast beautiful-colored dots of light all over the art room. "It's my new prism."

"Prison?" Sara asked.

"Prism. It refracts light."

"Refracts?"

"It takes a light beam and redirects it. It makes longer and shorter wavelengths so that it projects different colors. I'm still reading up on exactly what is happening in this amazing piece of glass, but I thought it would be useful to my art students to help them better understand colors and the natural blending of them."

Sara was so excited she thought she would jump out of her skin. "Vibrations," she said under her breath.

"Yes," the teacher said, softly studying the intensity of her new little friend. "Are you an artist?"

"Me? Oh no. I'm not good at that at all."

"You might be surprised," Miss Ralph said. "I'll bet you are full of artistic talent that you don't even know you have. Maybe before long I'll see you in one of my classes."

Bang! Sara and Miss Ralph both jumped as Seth blasted through the classroom door.

"Sorry."

"Seth!" Sara said in surprise.

"Sara!" Seth said in surprise, too. Then, walking to the window and reaching out to touch the shining object spinning in the window, he asked, "What is *this?*"

Miss Ralph stood back, wide-eyed, wondering what in the world was going on here. Who were these inquisitive children, so full of enthusiasm for her new prism?

"It's a prism," Sara said proudly. "It refracts light."

"I had no idea this prism was going to attract so much attention. I should have thought of this a long time ago," Miss Ralph said. She then explained to Seth what she had told Sara, and then they thanked her and left her classroom.

Sara and Seth could hardly wait to get out into the hallway where they could talk in private.

"Can you believe that we would both end up in Miss Ralph's room the first thing in the morning? This *Law of Attraction* thing is spooky," Seth said.

"Do you think everyone will notice it, or do you think we're the only vibrational matches to the prism?" asked Sara.

"I have an idea it was there just for us."

"Me, too," Sara said. "This is going to be a fun day."

Seth held the door open and they went outside. As they were walking down the front steps, they heard the town siren blaring off in the distance. This little town had no official fire department. There was only one very old fire truck that was kept in a garage on Main Street. Whenever there was a fire in the community, a loud siren was sounded; and volunteers, from as far as the sound would carry, would quickly come to help put out the blaze. It rarely sounded, but when it did it always stirred a great deal of interest and action.

"I wonder what *that's* about," Sara said, standing and squinting off into the distance.

"Shush, listen," Seth said, holding his finger up to his lips.

"It's the fire siren," Sara explained.

"I know that, but what else do you hear?"

Sara stopped walking, trying to hear what Seth was talking about.

Sara grinned. "Howling. I hear howling. Every dog in town must be howling. Geez, Seth, is this weird or what? The day hasn't even begun, and already we've had two amazing vibrational experiences."

"I just hope it isn't *my* house burning down again, Seth said, laughing.

"That's not funny, Seth," Sara said. "And I'm beginning to think we shouldn't spend much time talking about *anything* we *don't* want. Things seem to be happening pretty quickly around here."

"See ya after school."

"Yeah, see ya."

CHAPTER 26
A Magical Vibrational Match

Sara yawned broadly, and halfway through her yawn, she remembered to cover her mouth. She looked around at her classmates to see if anyone had noticed, but no one seemed to. She looked at her watch, wishing that the day would pass more quickly so that she could meet with Seth and talk about all the things she had on her list. In only one day, one of her teachers had talked about Beethoven, the deaf music composer; and Helen Keller, the amazing woman who was blind as well as deaf . . . Sara couldn't remember a day where more things that had to do with the five senses had been discussed. She could hardly wait to meet up with Seth to compare notes.

All of a sudden a truly awful odor reached Sara's nose. "Ooooo, yuck!" Sara exclaimed, clapping her hand over her mouth and nose. At the same time, other students were covering their faces, coughing, and gasping at the pungent odor.

"Well," Mr. Jorgenson said and smiled. "It's been quite a while since I've smelled *that* fragrance."

"What is that awful smell?" Sara called out.

"Well, if my memory serves me right, I'd say that some rascals over in the science lab have cooked up another batch of rotten-egg gas. And somehow they've managed to get it into the ventilation system."

Sara wondered how Mr. Jorgensen knew so much so fast about this awful smell. She couldn't help but think, from the twinkle she saw in his eye, that he'd cooked up a batch or two of that himself in his younger days.

Then the sound-system speaker in the classroom crackled, as it always did when the principal was about to make an announcement. "Attention. This is Mr. Marchant. It seems we are experiencing a rather unfortunate incident in the eighth-grade chemistry lab. There's no danger present—except to those responsible for this prank, that is."

Sara laughed.

"This will conclude the school session for today. Teachers are advised to dismiss their classes now. Bus-riding students may assemble in the loading area in half an hour. All other students may leave the campus now. That's all."

Sara leaped from her chair. She was joyous amidst all the hacking and coughing. *Whoops, better not look too happy,* Sara thought. *They'll think I was in on it.*

I probably am in on it, in some way, Sara thought. *This Law of Attraction stuff is weird.*

Sara left the building with a herd of other students. She searched the crowd, hoping to meet up with Seth so that they could begin comparing notes. And there was Seth standing by the flagpole, scanning the crowd for Sara. She smiled. "I'm glad you waited. What have *you* got?"

"Geez, Sara, I feel like we've stepped into the *Twilight Zone.* How is it possible that so many unusual things could happen in one day, and that the day just happens to be the one after Solomon gave us an assignment about the very same thing?"

"I know. Do you think Solomon is behind all of this?"

"It must be something like that, Sara. This has just been the most amazing day I've ever lived." Seth opened his notebook and began to read.

"First, there was the prism thing," Sara blurted, too eager to wait for Seth's first notation.

"Well, for me, that was the second thing," Seth said. "I sort of stepped in something bad, cutting across Mrs. Thompson's lawn, on my way to school."

Sara burst out laughing. Mrs. Thompson had five big dogs. Sara had stopped cutting across *her* lawn years ago.

"Then the prism thing with Miss Ralph . . . then the sirens."

"Uh-huh."

"Then, in P.E., there's this really irritating high-pitched squealing sound. We all heard it, but nobody could figure out what it was. It was the feedback from Mr. Jewkes's hearing aid. Did you know Mr. Jewkes wears a hearing aid? Well, he does, and he had it in his pocket instead of in his ear, so *he* couldn't hear it. Meanwhile, the rest of us are going nuts."

Sara giggled. "What else?"

Sara and Seth walked rapidly toward the tree house as Seth continued to turn the pages in his small notebook. They both were filled with a delicious eagerness to share the events of their separate days.

"Well, that's the high point for me. Except for that disgusting smell that closed the school. What in the world was that?"

"Mr. Jorgensen said it was rotten-egg gas from the chemistry lab that a few students somehow got into the ventilation system."

"Nice." Seth smiled.

Sara couldn't tell if that was a good nice or a bad nice. She didn't think Seth would ever do anything destructive or anything that would cause such a major inconvenience to so many people.

"Ya gotta hand it to 'em. They know how to close down a school," Seth added. "They'll probably grow up to be politicians."

Sara couldn't tell if that was a good thing or a bad thing.

"I guess it takes all kinds," Seth added.

She couldn't tell if Seth thought these were good kinds or bad kinds.

Sara couldn't stand it any longer. "What about it, Seth? Would *you* ever put rotten-egg gas in the ventilation ducts?"

Seth was quiet . . . Sara felt uneasy; she hoped that Seth would say, "No, I would never do anything like that." Sara didn't really like all of the rules. And much of what adults had decided, she had concluded at times, was pretty stupid. But when it came down to it, Sara believed in keeping promises and rules, and she didn't believe in causing trouble for others—even if they deserved it.

"Nah, *I* wouldn't do it," Seth responded.

Sara felt relief.

"I don't much care for people who deliberately make trouble for others."

"Me either," Sara added, smiling.

"What's on *your* list?" Seth asked.

"Well, I've got some of the same things you do, like the prism and the sirens and the dogs howling. We saw a film about Helen Keller. That was pretty amazing. Did you know that she couldn't see *or* hear?"

"Bummer," Seth said.

"In science class, there's this sound: *eeekk, eeek, eeek.* It sounded like it was squeaking in the walls or something. Mrs. Thompson was just going nuts, running all around the room trying to figure out where it was coming from. She was standing on chairs, putting her ear to the wall. It was wild."

"What happened?" Seth asked.

"First, she called the janitor, who must be as deaf as Mr. Jewkes because *he* couldn't hear it at all; and then the maintenance man from the bus garage came in, and he climbed up on all the chairs, and *he* couldn't figure it out either. And then she asked me to gather up the papers from everyone's desk, and when I put the papers on *her* desk, I could hear the sound really loud. It sounded like it was coming from near her desk. So I told them, 'Hey, it sounds to me like it's coming from over here.'"

"What was it?"

"It was her timer, you know, like a kitchen timer? It was in her briefcase, getting squashed or something, and it was beeping its head off. Mrs. Thompson was so embarrassed."

Seth laughed hard. "That's the best one yet!"

"What a great day! I've smelled more things today, both good and bad, than I can remember in a whole year. I've heard and seen more odd things than I can ever remember. You don't think this is going to keep up, and that tomorrow we'll get our fingerprints sanded off and find ground glass in our lunch, do you?"

Seth laughed. "Well, so far, it's been relatively painless. I can't wait to hear what Solomon has to say about all this."

Seth and Sara climbed the ladder to the tree house and waited for Solomon. Sometimes he was already there, but recently, he had been making some rather dramatic entrances after they arrived.

"What I most want Solomon to explain is how it's possible that all of these weird things are happening in *one* day. Is he doing it to show us?"

Whoooooosh. Solomon dived down into the tree and landed hard on the platform that Seth and Sara were standing on.

Good afternoon, my fine featherless friends. I trust you have had an enjoyable day.

"It was an amazing day, Solomon," Sara began. "You just won't believe what has happened."

Oh, I think I might. Solomon smiled.

"So, you *did* do it, Solomon. You arranged all of these weird things for us to learn more about our physical senses, didn't you?" Sara asked with a grin.

I have no idea what you are talking about. Solomon smiled back.

"Yeah, *right*," Sara quipped. "I just knew you were behind it."

Sara, I assure you that I am not the creator of your experience. I cannot project things into your experience. Only you can do that. There is no Law of Assertion, only the <u>Law of Attraction.</u>

Sara scowled. Somehow she had rather liked the idea of Solomon arranging all of these magical events in their day. She actually felt a bit disappointed that he wouldn't take the credit.

Seth was quiet. Sara could see, by the serious look on his face, that he was deep in thought.

Seth began, "So, Solomon, are you saying that you had nothing to do with any of this?"

Well, Solomon smiled, *I may have influenced you toward your attraction. As the three of us talked about the physical senses, we formed a focal point of energy around that subject. I certainly was instrumental in helping you focus and, therefore, offer your vibration about the subject of the physical senses. But it was the vibration that you two were offering that was responsible for the things you attracted.*

"But Solomon, how can that be? Are you saying that just by listening to you and talking about the five senses, *we made all of those things happen?*"

Not entirely. The art teacher had long been planning to buy that prism. She just hadn't gotten around to it. Your interest in the sense of sight added just enough influence to her plan, which was already set into motion,

*to give her the impulse to go ahead and act on her idea.
The same with the clever chemists who brewed up the
batch of rotten-egg gas. They had been planning that for
weeks. Your focus added just enough impetus to set that
one in motion as well.*

*In fact, all of those things were about to happen,
and many of them would have happened anyway with
or without your influence. <u>But without your attention to
them, you would not have been in a vibrational position
to rendezvous with the outcome.</u>*

Seth's eyes shined bright with understanding.

"So my impulse to cut across Mrs. Thompson's
yard was inspired by our conversation."

*That is correct. How many students do you think
burst into the art room to take a look at that prism?*

"How many?" Sara asked eagerly.

Two, Solomon replied. *Only you two, who had
achieved a vibrational match with that.*

"I get it," Sara blurted. "So all of those things
were already out there happening, or getting ready
to happen, and our attention just made us meet up
with them!"

That's right. Solomon smiled.

"And if they're already teetering on the verge
of happening, our attention pushes them over the
top?" Seth added.

Right again, Solomon agreed.

"Geez, Solomon, do you understand how much
power that means we have?"

Indeed, I do.

Seth and Sara sat quietly, nearly stunned by this new revelation.

"I guess we can pretty much do good stuff or bad stuff with this power," Seth added.

That's true, Solomon said. *Just remember that in either case, you'll be right in the middle of it.*

"Oh, yeah." Seth laughed. "That's something to think about, isn't it?"

Sara and Seth laughed. Neither Seth nor Sara nor Solomon believed that any of them would ever do anything to make anyone else uncomfortable.

"The *Law of Attraction* sure is interesting," Seth said.

"You can say that again," Sara agreed, sitting back against the tree and sighing heavily under the weight of this awesome new revelation.

Be easy about all of this, Solomon said. *Practice directing your thoughts and watch how quickly your real-life experience reflects whatever you have imagined.*

Let the Universe show you, by what comes back into your experience, what the primary content of your thoughts is. We'll talk more tomorrow. And so, my vibrational friends, I'll be off and let you work your magic. Have fun with this. And with that, Solomon was gone.

Sara and Seth sat quietly, both deep in their own thoughts.

"Is this fun or what!" Sara exclaimed.

"This is great!"

Solomon made one more low, swift pass past the tree house.

Seth and Sara burst into laughter. "There's never a dull moment around here," Seth said.

"I just love it!"

CHAPTER 27

Life Is Wonderful

Sara waited in the tree house for Seth and Solomon. She felt uncomfortable. It was unusual not to have crossed paths with Seth at school, and she wondered if maybe he hadn't been there today.

"Where is everybody?" Sara impatiently spoke out loud. This felt weird.

Sara had left her book bag at the foot of the tree, and she thought about climbing down and bringing it back up. But she really felt too fitful to do any reading or homework. Something was wrong; she could just feel it.

Solomon glided in softly and landed on the platform with Sara. Before he could offer his usual "Isn't this a beautiful day?" Sara blurted, "Solomon, where's Seth?"

He'll be along soon. I suspect that he has had a rather interesting day.

"Is something wrong?"

Are things usually wrong when they are interesting?

"Well, no, but I don't think he came to school today. At least, I didn't see him all day."

Are things usually wrong when they are different from usual? Is it possible that things could be different and still be all right?

There was logic in what Solomon was saying, but Sara felt uneasy. While it was true that she hadn't known Seth very long, he had shown some rather stable patterns, and Sara had become comfortable with his predictable patterns of behavior.

Seth burst through the trees and began climbing up the ladder.

"Oh, good," Sara said quietly. "Solomon, don't tell him I was worried, okay?" She felt silly for worrying.

Your secret is safe with me. However, the <u>Law of Attraction</u> is not so good at keeping secrets.

Sara looked at Solomon, wishing she could ask what he meant by that, but Seth had bounded up onto the platform.

"Hi, guys, what's up?"

"Nothing much," Sara answered, trying to appear calm and cool. "Just waiting for you."

"Oh, sorry," Seth said.

Sara waited for some explanation about where he had been.

Seth fidgeted with a twig, cleaning leaves from

the cracks in the platform. He seemed intensely involved in it and didn't look up.

Something is wrong, Sara thought.

I'll be right back, Solomon said, flying out of the tree house and out over the river. Sara and Seth stood up, watching Solomon. *This is weird,* Sara thought. *What's going on around here?*

Solomon swooped down and took the heavy rope in his beak and flew the rope back up to the platform. And what happened next left Sara and Seth standing in amazement with their mouths hanging open: Holding tightly to the rope with his claws, Solomon jumped off the platform and swung way out across the river as Sara and Seth had done hundreds of times before.

Geronimooo! Solomon called out as his feathers blew straight back in the wind. Sara and Seth laughed hard.

Solomon made his dismount, not different from theirs, and landed on the riverbank. Then he flew out across the river, caught the rope in his beak, and flew back up to the platform. Seth took the rope from Solomon.

That is an exhilarating experience, indeed! Solomon began.

Sara and Seth stood puzzled, neither one knowing what to say.

Finally Sara said, "Solomon, whatever would you find exhilarating about swinging from a dumb tree rope when you can fly anywhere you want anytime you want?"

Hearing how her words sounded, she looked quickly at Seth and said, "Sorry, Seth, I don't mean that the rope is dumb, I mean, it's real neat, but . . ."

"I know what you meant, Sara. I was about to ask the same question. We swing because *we* can't fly. Well, not usually, that is. But why would you—"

Solomon interrupted. *There are no best experiences. Flying is not better than swinging, and swinging isn't better than walking. Each experience has its own benefits. It's the variation that makes life full and delicious and interesting.*

For me, today, the swing was a first-time experience. I have never before put my faith in the strength or trajectory of a rope hanging from a tree. The thrill continues to be in the new discovery.

"Gee, Solomon, I didn't think that you were having new experiences," Seth said. "I keep thinking that you know everything."

How perfectly boring that would be. We are all continuing to expand. We are eternally in a joyous state of becoming.

"I've been thinking that all I want to do is close my eyes and fly with Solomon. I want to leave this boring town behind and explore all the wonderful things that are out there," Sara said.

It is a normal thing, Sara, to be thrilled with the newness of an experience. I am certain that your first flying experiences with me were as exhilarating for you as my first swing on your rope was for me. But I assure you, you did not come forth into this glorious physical body, and into this magnificent physical experience, only to yearn to get out of it. In fact, you knew that the greatest thrills are right here, in your body, on this wonderful planet Earth, interacting with others and constantly discovering new things to think about and new people to interact with. It is all here for you. And it is wonderful.

Seth and Sara were both filled with a joyful feeling of well-being. While they couldn't fully understand what Solomon was telling them, they could feel, by the intensity of his words, that it was true.

Something about seeing this magical bird, who they knew could do anything imaginable, taking such great delight in the simple pleasure of swinging from their tree-house rope helped them understand that where they were standing, in the middle of their plain physical world, was not such a bad place to be.

"So, Solomon, are you saying that we won't be flying with you anymore, or that we shouldn't want to fly?"

You may do anything that you want to do. I want to guide you to a recognition of the enormous value of where you now stand. So many people are feeling dissatisfied with what is around them, spending all of their time reaching for things that feel out of their grasp, when there is so much pleasure and value for them if they were to look around, right where they now stand.

I do not want to guide you toward or away from anything. I want you to know that your options are unlimited and that it is in the new experience that your greatest joy will always come. You are expanding Beings, ever-expanding Beings. When you understand that and allow it—and even encourage it—you will always find your greatest joy.

Sara smiled. She was beginning to understand what Solomon was up to.

"So what is predictable or already known isn't necessarily the best thing. Is that what you're saying, Solomon?"

Expect your lives to be predictably wonderful as you continually explore new experiences. This is a wonderful life you're living, my friends, and I just want you to know that.

"I do, Solomon," Sara said softly, feeling Solomon's love wrapping around her and through her.

"Me, too," Seth said softly. "Me, too."

CHAPTER 28

There's No Injustice

"**S**olomon," Sara continued, "what did you mean when you said that the *Law of Attraction* doesn't keep secrets?"

When you are feeling something, even though you may pretend that you don't feel it by saying words that are different from what you are feeling, the <u>Law of Attraction</u> is still responding to your feeling. And so, the things that come to you in response to your feeling always point out what that feeling is.

"Hmm." Sara was quiet. Solomon's words sounded the same as other things he had told her before.

If you feel vulnerable or afraid, but you pretend that you are not afraid—sometimes even by seeming aggressive, or like a bully yourself—still, the <u>Law of Attraction</u> brings you experience after experience that matches your feeling of vulnerability.

If you feel sorry for yourself, even though you may

185

pretend otherwise, the way you are treated by others con-
tinues to match the way you really feel.

If you feel poor—you cannot attract prosperity.

If you feel fat—you cannot attract slenderness.

If you feel unfairly treated—you cannot attract fairness.

Sara scowled. She had heard things like this from Solomon before, but a part of her continued to believe that all of this was really unfair.

"But Solomon, that just doesn't seem right. It seems like the *Law of Attraction* should be a little more helpful and give you a break, I mean, when you really need one."

Solomon smiled. *That's the thing that most people misunderstand about the <u>Law of Attraction.</u> They think the <u>Law of Attraction</u> should behave like a parent or a friend who would see a friend in trouble and bend over backward to help out.*

"Well, that would be nicer, don't you think?"

Actually, Sara, I think that would make matters worse.

"How come?"

Because, if the <u>Law of Attraction</u> were inconsistent, no one would ever be able to find their place within it. But because it is always precisely consistent, in time and with practice, everyone can learn how to attract exactly what they desire.

You see, Sara, if you carefully observe the way you are feeling, and then you notice that what comes to you *matches that feeling, you then begin to understand how the <u>Law of Attraction</u> works. Then you realize that by changing the way you feel, you can change how things turn out.*

"But Solomon, what if I can't change the way I feel?"

Well, Sara, there would never be a reason for that.

"I mean, like, what if something really *awful* happened?"

Well, I would suggest that you turn your attention away from that and turn it toward something that would make you feel better.

"But I mean, what if it was really, really awful?"

All the more reason to turn to something else.

"But—" Sara protested.

Solomon interrupted. *Sara, people often believe that they can make things better by getting right in the middle of something awful and working hard to fix it. But that is never what makes things better. What makes things better is to give your attention to things that make you feel better—because what is coming to you is coming because of what you are feeling.*

"I know you keep telling me this, Solomon, but it's just that..."

Most people are going about it the hard way, Sara. Try to control how you are feeling and see how much easier it all becomes.

It turns out that there is no such thing as injustice.

Everyone always gets exactly what they are feeling or offering. It is always a match—and therefore, it is always fair.

"Okay, Solomon." Sara sighed. She knew that Solomon was right. She also knew there was no point in trying to convince Solomon otherwise. He never wavered when he talked about the *Law of Attraction.*

And there was something about that that had a nice ring to it: *No such thing as injustice.* Something about that felt quite good.

As Sara walked to school, she continued to ponder what she and Solomon had talked about: *If you feel poor—you can't attract prosperity. If you feel fat—you can't attract slenderness. If you feel unfairly treated—you cannot attract fairness.*

"That's *so* unfair," Sara heard the girls behind her complaining. Sara smiled. She was always amazed at how often the very thing she was speaking about or thinking about turned up in her experience in some way. She couldn't hear them well enough to know what was wrong, but it was obvious they were feeling it strongly.

You can't get there from there, Sara thought.

"That's not fair, that's not fair," Sara heard a boy's voice protesting. Mr. Marchant had a firm grip on a squirming and angry student as he marched him up the steps of the administration building.

"Life's not usually fair, young man."

"Well, how come you let the others go?" the young boy whined.

Mr. Marchant did not answer his young prisoner.

"Oh man, this always happens to me."

Sara smiled. *There is no such thing as injustice,* she remembered.

"Hey, Sara, wait up!"

Sara turned to see Seth running to catch up with her. "Sara, I need to talk to you. Something awful has happened."

Sara gulped and waited for Seth to catch his breath. It seemed like an hour before he began to speak.

"*What?!* What *is* it?"

"My dad found out about the tree house and says I can't go there anymore. He says there are more important things for me to be doing than messing around in a tree."

"Oh, Seth," Sara whined. "That's not fair."

As Sara heard the words come out of her mouth, she stammered over them. She knew about the *Law of Attraction,* and she knew that the way you feel affects what comes to you. She knew—or was coming to know—all of that. But how in the world could anyone not feel the unfairness of what Seth was telling her?

"He said Mr. Wilsenholm came into the hardware

store complaining that some kids were swinging from his trees. He said that it's trespassing and dangerous and if he has to, he'll cut the trees down to keep the hooligans out of them. He said they could break their necks and kill themselves.

"My dad knew it was me 'cause he knows how I like tree houses. He says I should've known better and he whip—"

"What?"

"Nothin', I gotta go."

Sara's eyes filled with tears. She made her way to her locker and dumped her books inside. She went into the girls' bathroom and wiped her face with a wet paper towel. "It's just not fair," she said out loud.

Remember, Sara, there is no such thing as injustice. Whatever comes to you always matches what you have been vibrating and feeling.

"I know you keep saying that, Solomon, but now what do I do?"

You must change how you feel.

"But it's too late for that. Seth's already been forbidden to go to the tree house, and Mr. Wilsenholm knows we've been there, so now I probably can't go either."

It's never too late, Sara. No matter what happens, you still have control over the way you feel. And since you still have control over the way you feel, you can still change the outcome, no matter how it seems now.

Sara wiped her face again. "Okay, Solomon. I'll try. Sure doesn't look like I have anything to lose by trying."

We'll visit in the tree house after school tonight.

"But Mr. Wilsenholm says that's trespassing."

Solomon didn't respond.

"Okay, I'll see ya there," Sara said just as the bathroom door banged open and a girl from Sara's classroom blasted in.

"See who *where?*" she said, turning around in a full circle, seeing that Sara was all alone in the bathroom.

"I don't know," Sara said, leaving the bathroom.

"Okay, *be* weird," the girl said.

"Okay, I *will.*" Sara smiled as she walked down the hall.

CHAPTER 29

Trusting the Law of Attraction

It had been a very long day at school, and Sara was so happy when the final bell rang. She waited for Seth for a few minutes by the flagpole, hoping that he would show up, but the whole time she was waiting, she really didn't think he'd be there. So Sara went to the tree house alone—first feeling sad, knowing that Seth wouldn't be there, then feeling angry that his father had forbidden him to go, and then feeling guilty that she was trespassing. What a mean word: *trespassing.*

Sara was happy to see that Solomon was sitting on the platform waiting for her.

Good afternoon, Sara. It's nice to have an opportunity to visit.

"Sure is, Solomon, but do you think I'll get in trouble for trespassing?"

That's a pretty strong word. How does it make you feel?

"Pretty bad, Solomon. I don't even know for sure what it means—but it sounds serious. I'm pretty sure it means I shouldn't be here. Do you think we're going to get in trouble?"

Well, Sara, all I can tell you is that I spend a great deal of time sitting in the tops of trees, and I have never gotten into trouble for trespassing.

Sara laughed. "Yeah, but Solomon, you're an *owl*. People expect to see *you* in trees."

But this tree doesn't belong to me any more than it belongs to you, Sara. Technically speaking, the birds or the cats or the squirrels, in fact, thousands of creatures who inhabit this tree right now, could be called trespassers.

Sara laughed. "Yeah, I guess that's right."

Mr. Wilsenholm doesn't mind sharing his beautiful trees with all of them, Sara. And I suspect that if he understood how at home you are in his tree—and what good care you are taking of yourself when you are in his tree—he wouldn't worry about your spending some time here either.

Sara felt a soothing sensation wash over her. It was the first relief from this awful feeling that she had felt all day.

"Really, Solomon, do you think so?"

I really do, Sara. Mr. Wilsenholm is not a mean man, selfishly wanting this tree all to himself. In fact, I believe he would be pleased if he understood how you feel about this beautiful old tree. I think he's just worrying about things that might happen. And because he does not know how responsible you are and how well you can handle yourself in his tree, he imagines the very worst thing happening. And then his feelings come about because of his imagined worry rather than from what is really happening.

"Well, what should I do?"

Well, Sara, if I were you, I'd go home tonight and think about how wonderful this old tree is. I'd think about how good it feels to be in the tree. I'd make a long list of the things you like most about it, remembering the fun you and Seth have had in the tree. Keep reliving the best parts, playing them over and over in your mind, until you are full and overflowing with the wonderful feeling of this tree—and then, trust the <u>Law of Attraction</u> to help out.

"Well, what will the *Law of Attraction* do?"

There are many things it could do. You never really know for sure until it happens. But one thing you do know: If you are feeling good, whatever happens will feel good, too.

"Okay, Solomon. I'll do that. It's easy to make lists of things I love about this tree. I *love* this tree."

Solomon smiled. *Indeed you do, Sara. Indeed you do.*

Sara lay in her bed that night thinking about her wonderful tree. She remembered how thrilled she had been when Seth first showed her the tree house, and the thrill of leaping off the platform, holding tightly to the rope Seth had tied to the big limb. She laughed as she remembered Seth tumbling into the bushes the first times she saw him jump from the rope, and she thought of the glorious hours she and Seth and Solomon had spent talking there. And with those lovely thoughts rolling across her mind, Sara fell asleep.

CHAPTER 30

A Trespassing Kitten

Sara opened her eyes, surprised that her bedroom was filled with sunlight. She was even more surprised to discover that it was nearly nine o'clock. She jumped out of bed, wondering how in the world her mother had allowed her to sleep and miss school. And then she remembered that today was Saturday.

"Well, hello, Sleepyhead," her mother said as Sara went into the kitchen. "You looked like you were enjoying your sleep so much I hated to wake you up. Did you have a good night's sleep?"

"Yes," Sara said, still a bit groggy.

"Daddy's working again today. I thought I'd drive into the city and do some shopping. Jason's spending the day with Billy. You're welcome to come with me if you'd like, or . . ."

Sara held her breath. Was her mother really going to allow her to spend the day at home, or wherever, alone?

". . . or whatever you'd like," her mother continued.

"I think I'll just stay here," Sara said, secretly jumping up and down inside.

"All right, sweetheart. I'll be back late in the afternoon. Have a good day, and don't worry about doing your Saturday chores. I've tidied up some and things are in pretty good shape. I'll see you later."

Sara was grinning from ear to ear. While her mother was nearly always pleasant, and Sara would readily admit that she lived a rather good life, still, this was good fortune up and beyond. Was Solomon's *Law of Attraction* working its magic so soon?

Sara got dressed, pulled a sweatshirt over her clothes, and went outside. She thought about the tree house and felt a very strong urge to go there and climb high into the tree house and *be*. But she felt an equally strong reluctance.

Then an idea filled her head. She had a clear image of crossing through the pasture behind the Wilsenholms' yard, traversing the river by way of the log crossing, and coming out near Main Street at her leaning perch at the river. The impulse was *so* strong that she bolted out the back door and raced across her backyard to the pasture.

As she climbed through the fence, she heard someone crying. She stood still to see if she could tell where it was coming from. She saw a woman in a bathrobe standing out under a big tree looking up into the branches. Sara recognized that she was looking into the back side of the Wilsenholm yard but wasn't sure who the woman was. Mrs. Wilsenholm had been very sick for many years, and Sara couldn't remember the last time she had seen her.

"Are you all right?" Sara called out.

"No, dear, I'm *not* all right. My cat seems to have stranded herself up in that tree again, and she's been there all night. My husband is out of town, and I just don't know *how* I'll ever get her down. Oh dear, I just don't know *what* to do." The woman wrung her hands and then clutched her robe around her body. Sara knew she must be uncomfortably chilly, and she was clearly upset.

Sara looked up into the giant tree. High in the tree was a very small cat. *Meow! Meow!* It certainly seemed frightened.

"Here, kitty, kitty, kitty," Sara called out.

"That's no use," Mrs. Wilsenholm said. "I've been calling her for hours."

"Mrs. Wilsenholm, you should go inside and get warm," Sara said calmly. "Don't worry about your cat. I'll get her down."

"Oh no, honey, I couldn't let you do that. You could fall and hurt yourself."

"I'll be all right. I'm very good in trees."

Mrs. Wilsenholm reluctantly went inside and watched Sara from her large living-room window.

Sara spied a ladder leaning up against the side of the barn and dragged it to the base of the tree. She walked the ladder up, rung by rung, until it was standing sturdily against the tree, and then she wiggled the ladder back and forth, digging its feet firmly into the soil at the base of the tree. She stepped up on the first step and jumped up and down to be sure that the ladder was stable. Then she cautiously began to climb it. The ladder wasn't very tall, but it did reach to the first large branch of the tree. Sara held on to the branch and lifted herself up from the ladder and up into the tree. Once on that branch, she could easily reach the next, and then the next, until Sara *and* the kitten were high in the tree.

The kitten looked frightened and wouldn't let go of the tree, so Sara sat on the branch trying to figure out what to do next. "Well, kitty, are *you* trespassing?" Sara asked.

The cat meowed.

"Oh, you *are*, are you?" Sara laughed. She sat comfortably on the big branch with her feet dangling down and quietly stroked the kitten while she softly explained how she really didn't believe the kitten was trespassing. And how there was nothing to be afraid of, and that it was almost as easy to climb *down* out of a tree as it was to climb *up* into one.

Sara finally tugged the kitten loose from the

tree and sat stroking its back until it relaxed and stopped meowing. She gently put it up under her sweatshirt, carefully tucking her sweatshirt into her pants, making a safe carrying pouch for her frightened little friend. And then Sara carefully made her way back down the tree and to the ladder and to the ground.

Mrs. Wilsenholm was waiting with a big smile when Sara reached the ground.

"That was the most amazing rescue I've ever seen!" she said, taking her kitten from Sara and holding it softly up against her neck. "What's *your* name?"

"I'm Sara. We live at the end of the street, by the dairy."

"Oh, I see. *Sara.* And you spend a lot of time in trees, do you?"

"Well, yeah, I guess." Sara smiled. "I've been climbing trees since I could walk. My mom used to worry, but she doesn't anymore. She says if I was going to fall on my head, I probably would've done it long before now."

"Well, from what I've just seen, I don't believe your mother has a thing in the world to worry about. You're an agile young girl, Sara, *and* you've saved my cat. I just don't know how to thank you.

"My husband has just been fit to be tied over some youngsters who've been climbing in those big trees back by the river. He's even threatening to cut them down. I keep telling him that he's making much too much of it, but he's a stubborn old man, and once he makes up his mind, he usually won't budge. But if *those* young ones are as good in trees as you are, he'd have nothing to worry about now, would he, Sara?"

"No, ma'am, he wouldn't." Sara hesitated, and then she blurted, "And I guess this is as good a time as any to tell you—it's my friend and I who've been climbing in your tree."

Sara gulped. She had said it before she'd really thought it through. It had seemed right at the time, but now Mrs. Wilsenholm was quiet.

"Well, I'll tell you what, Sara. I'm going to tell Mr. Wilsenholm what I've seen here today. I can't promise anything because he's a stubborn old fool, but occasionally he still listens to me. I'll work on him for you. If he could see you up in that tree, I don't think he'd be so worried about you. Give me a little time. Stop by in a few days and I'll let you know what he says."

"Thank you, oh thank you, thank you!" Sara gasped. She wasn't sure what was more exciting: the possibility of them actually being permitted to play in the tree or the miracle that the *Law of Attraction* had provided. In either case, Sara was elated.

CHAPTER 31

We Can Do It

Sara was headed back toward home from her kitten-saving experience with Mrs. Wilsenholm before she remembered she had been on her way to her leaning perch. *I wish there were some way I could tell Seth the good news,* Sara thought.

Sara had never been in Seth's house, and even though Seth hadn't really said much about his life at home, Sara could tell by what he didn't say that things were not very pleasant there. And so, she knew she shouldn't just show up on his doorstep.

"I wish I could run into him somehow," Sara said out loud.

She stopped at the side of the river and gazed out at her crossing log. She stepped up onto the log and held her arms out at her sides to find her balance, and then she literally ran across the log. She felt so wonderful. With the miracle that had just happened, she felt as if she could fly across the river.

"Hey, young lady, don't you know this river is dangerous and that you could drown?" Sara heard Seth's teasing voice coming from the bushes. He was sitting on a big rock only a few feet from the end of the crossing log. His shoes and socks were in a heap beside him, and both feet were dangling in the cold water.

"Seth, I'm so glad to see you! You'll never guess what happened!"

Seth could tell by her intensity that something significant had happened. "Tell me! What *is* it?"

"I was cutting across the Wilsenholms' back-yard—"

"Geez, Sara, you're brave. I thought . . ."

"I know, I know. I wasn't really thinking about what I was doing . . . but it turned out really well.

"Mrs. Wilsenholm was in her backyard crying. Her little kitten was stuck really high up in a tree. So I said I could get it down, but she said I shouldn't try because it was dangerous. But I told her I would be all right, and she didn't stop me . . . so I climbed up in the tree and got her kitten down . . . and then she said that her husband was angry because kids were climbing in his trees, but if those kids were as good in the trees as I was, he probably wouldn't worry about them so much . . . so I told her I was one of the kids who had been climbing in their trees . . ."

Sara gasped for a breath of air. She had been talking so fast she was barely breathing.

"Sara! What were you *thinking?*"

"No, Seth, it's okay. She was so relieved that I saved her cat, and so impressed with how safe she could see I was in the tree, she said she would talk to her husband and try to convince him that we're really safe in his trees."

"Do you think she can *do* it, Sara? Will he listen to her?"

"I don't know. But something magical is happening, Seth. Solomon said to remember how wonderful it is to be in the tree, and that the *Law of Attraction* would help us. So last night I made a long list of everything I love about the tree house. And then this morning, it seemed like everything worked out to help that: My mother went shopping and said I could stay home and do as I please. That's a miracle in itself. And then she said that I didn't have to do my Saturday chores because she'd already finished what really needed to be done. I can't remember the last time *that* happened. I don't think that has ever happened before. And then there was Mrs. Wilsenholm out in her yard, crying over her stranded little cat. That was weird. Seth, it really feels like things are actually lining up to help us. Solomon has been talking about stuff like this for as long as I've known him, but I've never seen it work out so perfectly or so fast. I guess it's because this is something that we really want."

"Okay, Sara, so *now* what do we do?"

"Well, I don't think we have to figure that out. Solomon says our work is only to find the feeling place of what we *do* want—and the *Law of Attraction* will do the work."

"Hmm." Seth was quiet.

Sara sat waiting for him to say something.

Seth seemed to have something he wanted to say, but he wasn't saying it.

"What?" Sara prodded. "What *is* it?" She could see Seth was bothered about something.

"I think we're moving."

"Moving! Moving *where?"*

"My dad lost his job. Mr. Bergheim's son dropped out of college, and his dad says *he's* going to do the job my dad's been doing. Sara, it's just not fair!"

Not fair. Those words triggered Sara's new understanding about fairness, and Solomon's words streamed back into her mind: *Most people are going about it the hard way, Sara. Try to control how you are feeling and see how much easier it all becomes. It turns out that there is no such thing as injustice. Everyone always gets exactly what they are feeling or offering. It is always a match—and therefore it is always fair.*

"Seth, Seth," Sara gasped, excitedly. "We can fix this."

"Sara, I don't see how— "

Sara interrupted him. "Really, Seth. We *can.* All we have to do is make a list of all the things we like about your living here, or about your father working at the hardware store—and the *Law of Attraction* will take care of it."

"Sara, how in the world are *we* going to convince Mr. Bergheim to let my dad keep his job?"

"That's not our work, Seth. Solomon says . . ."

Leaves fluttered down from the tree overhead as Solomon executed a soft and perfect landing.

I thought I might find you two here, Solomon said, dropping down to the lowest limb and straightening his feathers with his beak. *This is a lovely day, isn't it?*

"Solomon, you won't believe all the things that have happened since I talked with you yesterday!" Sara blurted.

Well, I think I might have an idea. Solomon smiled.

Sara grinned, remembering that Solomon knew everything.

I see things are progressing nicely on the tree-house issue, Solomon spoke in a professor-like voice. *Now, let's go to work on this newest development.*

"Solomon, my dad lost his job. He says he's going to get a farm so he doesn't have to depend on the whims of some boss who'd rather have his irresponsible son working for him than an adult who'll run his business right."

I see, Solomon said. *It's natural for your father to feel bitter, under these conditions,* Solomon continued. *But feeling that way cannot help things. It can only make things worse. And it's perfectly natural for you to feel bitter about it, Seth, since it is affecting your life as well. And it's natural for you to feel bitter about it, too, Sara, because now it is affecting your life.*

"But what can *we* do, Solomon?" Sara blurted. "Isn't there something that we can do?"

Oh yes, indeed, Sara. You have much more power to positively affect things than you realize.

"But Solomon, we're just kids, how can we—?"

Solomon interrupted Seth. *One who is connected to the Stream is more powerful than a million who are not.*

Seth and Sara sat staring at each other. "You mean, we can make someone do something that they don't want to do?"

Not exactly. And it isn't your work to figure out what will be done or how it needs to be done. Your work is to imagine a happy outcome for everyone—and the Law of Attraction will bring it about.

"What do you mean, *for everyone?* You mean, for mean old Bergheim and his son?"

Seth, your bitterness may be natural under the circumstances, but it does not serve you well. Remember, when you feel angry or bitter, you are not connected to the Stream of Well-being. And when you are not connected to the Stream, your power of influence becomes insignificant.

Seth was quiet. He knew that Solomon had spoken about this many times.

Don't try to figure out how it will happen. Just pretend that this trauma has passed and all is well. Pretend that you and Sara are continuing to meet in the tree house and that your life is getting better and better. Find some thoughts that are pleasant and easy to find, and hold them in your mind. And when the other thoughts come, and they will for a while, just relax and release them—and focus again on the thoughts that feel better. And watch what happens.

"Solomon, are you going to help us?" Sara asked.

Help will come from endless places and will turn up in endless ways. You will be amazed at how much assistance you will receive to help you with your desire. But first you must be a match to your desire.

Sara and Seth looked at each other. They knew about vibrational matches; they remembered the artroom prism and the rotten-egg gas and the fire whistle blowing . . . they both were feeling much better.

"We can do it!" they both said at the same time. Then they both laughed.

You can, indeed, Solomon said.

"Solomon?" Sara asked. "You know how you've been telling us that the Universe answers our vibration? And that the *Law of Attraction* does the work? Well, does it work faster if it's about something that we really care about? I mean, like, with the tree house, it seems like magical things began happening really fast."

It always happens fast, Sara, whether it is seemingly big or small. It is as easy to create a castle as a button.

Have fun with it. Do your best to imagine a happy outcome. Don't try to figure out how it will happen. Skip over how it will happen, who will help, when it will happen, or where. Focus on what you really want and why you want it. And most of all, reach for a feeling of relief. All is well here.

Sara and Seth watched Solomon lift off and fly up into the sky. They sat quietly . . . each thinking about their future.

"I don't know where to start." Seth sighed. "Every time I try to think of something, I think of something bad."

"I know," Sara said. "Me, too. Maybe if we think of a bad thing that happened then we can think of the opposite."

"What do you mean?"

"Well, we could think of what it felt like when your dad came home and said he'd lost his job— and then we could pretend the opposite."

"I see what you mean. . . . Okay, I'm sitting upstairs in my room and I hear the front door bang shut, and I can hear my dad's voice in the kitchen . . ."

"How does he sound? Is he happy?"

"Yeah." Seth grinned. "He *is*. He's *real* happy and now I can hear my mother's voice, and she sounds happy, too. I run down the stairs, and I see them hugging, and my mother is wiping her face with her handkerchief."

"What do you think happened?" Sara asked, playing along with Seth's vision.

"Solomon says we don't have to figure out all the details, just the happy ending."

"Well, *that* feels good."

"Yeah."

"I sure hope this works," Sara said.

"Me, too. Anyway, I do feel better."

"Me, too."

"I better get going."

"Yeah, me, too."

"Seth!" Sara called back over her shoulder. "If your dad and mom aren't happy tonight, now you can remember our version instead of theirs. You know what I mean?"

"I do. I think I'll go to bed early. It'll be easier to imagine them happy if I'm not looking at their sad faces."

"Yeah." Sara laughed. "Good idea."

"Seth!" Sara called out again. "I really *do* believe it's going to be all right. I have a really good feeling about all of this."

"Yeah! See ya."

CHAPTER 32

It Works

"Sara, telephone!" her mother called from the kitchen. Sara poked her head out from her bedroom and asked, "Who is it?"

"It's Mrs. Wilsenholm, Sara. Why is Mrs. Wilsenholm calling *you?*"

"Oh, I don't know. Maybe 'cause I helped her find her kitten." Sara picked up the phone and pulled the long cord as far away from her mother as she could without it being too obvious that she didn't want her mother to overhear.

"Sara, I have some very good news for you. Mr. Wilsenholm has decided not to cut down the trees. But he says he wants to meet you. And your friend, too. Can you stop by after school today?"

"Okay," Sara said, trying to keep her voice calm to conceal her enthusiasm.

Sara hung up the telephone and walked toward her bedroom.

"Sara, what was *that* about?" Her mother sounded suspicious.

"Oh, nothing. Mrs. Wilsenholm just asked me to stop by her house after school today. It's okay, isn't it?"

"Well, I suppose so," her mother answered.

Once inside her bedroom, Sara bounded onto her bed. She jumped up and down with excitement, holding her hand over her mouth to keep from yelping.

It works! It works! It works! she yelped (in her mind).

Sara could barely contain herself. She wanted so much to find Seth and tell him the good news about the trees and about their appointment with Mr. Wilsenholm.

Sara hurried up the country road to the school grounds. She sat on the rock wall at the side of the administration building where she could get a good view of the front entrance and the flagpole and waited for Seth. She watched carloads of kids being dropped off and hoards of them walking through the front gates, but no Seth.

Where is he? Sara was beginning to feel worried.

What if his family really is moving and they're making him help them load the truck?

Sara shuddered. *That* was a perfectly awful thought.

As that strong uncomfortable feeling enveloped Sara, she remembered what Solomon had said: *You cannot get to a happy ending on an unhappy journey. Worry and well-being are opposite vibrations; well-being cannot come when you are in the feeling-place of worry.*

"I know, I know," Sara said out loud.

"Know *what?*" Seth said, coming up behind Sara and startling her.

"Geez, Seth, you scared me to death. What in the world are you doing behind the building?"

"Oh, I don't know. Sometimes I leave early and walk around the long way. Just felt like taking my time this morning."

Sara felt as if Seth were about to describe the tension at his house, but she smiled as she realized that he was deliberately *not* putting words to, or as Solomon would say, *adding power to,* this negative situation.

"Seth, I've got great news. Mrs. Wilsenholm called me last night and says her husband has decided not to cut down our trees, but he wants to meet me, and you, too. She asked us to stop by their house after school. I can. Can you?"

"Yeah, I guess I can. Sara, this is *great!*"

The bell rang, and they both felt disappointed to be pulled away from their happy topic.

They walked across the lawn and onto the sidewalk. "I wonder why he wants to meet *us?*" Seth pondered.

"I don't know."

"Well, I'll see ya. By the crossing log?"

"Yeah. Imagine a happy outcome!" Sara called over her shoulder.

"Yeah. You, too."

CHAPTER 33

Whose Tree House?

Sara struggled to keep her mind on what was happening in her classes. It felt like a very long day. She tried to imagine what Mr. Wilsenholm wanted to talk with them about, but every time she thought about meeting him, her heart would race and she'd lose her place in her thought.

He was a large man, and while Sara had seen him around town many times, she had never actually spoken to him. He was well known in the community and owned one of the largest farms; Sara wasn't sure which of the many pastures out in the valley belonged to him, but she was aware that he owned quite a lot of land.

Finally, again and again, Sara would come around to the easy-to-find thought of swinging in the tree with Seth. She always enjoyed remembering his first dismount from the rope—and his first perfect landing.

It's amazing how much pleasure you can get by just remembering the same happy moment over and over again, Sara thought, and goosebumps rose up all over her body.

When the bell rang, she jumped about a foot. She bolted from the classroom, dropped all of her books off in her locker, and ran out the front gates toward the crossing log.

Seth was already there waiting for her when she got there. They were both out of breath—and grinning.

"Well, here goes. Let's find out what's up," Sara said.

They walked up the long lane to the front door of the Wilsenholm house. Sara couldn't help but notice how really lovely everything looked from inside this yard. Large trees shaded the long path in, and delicate grass grew between the pretty flat stones that made up the walkway.

They banged the big brass knocker on the front door and waited.

Mrs. Wilsenholm came to the door with a welcoming smile on her face. "Sara, thank you for coming. And who is *this* nice young man?"

"I'm Seth. Seth Morris. Pleased to meet you."

Sara smiled. Seth seemed stiff and formal. She thought that if he had been wearing a hat, he would have tipped it about now.

"Come in and sit down. I made cookies for

you. I don't suppose your mothers would mind, do you?"

"No. That's very nice of you."

"Make yourselves comfortable. I'll get the cookies. Mr. Wilsenholm should be here any minute."

Sara and Seth sat awkwardly on the big sofa. This was the prettiest home Sara had ever been inside, and she could see by the way Seth was looking around that it wasn't a usual experience for him either.

They heard a car door slam shut as Mrs. Wilsenholm came into the room with the cookies. "Ah, there he is, right on time as usual. He'll wash his hands I imagine, and he'll be right in. Go ahead, eat some cookies. I'll be right back."

Sara bit into her cookie. She was sure it was delicious, but she wasn't really in the mood for it. Her mind was whirling and her heart was racing. "I haven't been this nervous since, since ever."

Seth laughed. "Me neither."

Mr. Wilsenholm charged into the room.

"Well, I'll be! You must be the famous Sara who climbs trees like you were born in them, and who rescues kittens."

Sara smiled and said, "Yes, sir."

"And who might *you* be?" Mr. Wilsenholm said, taking Seth's hand and heartily shaking it.

"Seth. Seth Morris, sir," Seth said, swallowing

hard. This was a powerful man, maybe the most powerful man Seth had ever seen up close.

"And did I understand correctly that you two are the ones who have been trespassing in my trees for the last several months?"

"Yes, sir," both Sara and Seth said in unison.

"I see." Mr. Wilsenholm sat down, staring at them intently.

"Who *tied* the rope up in that tree?"

"I did, sir."

"And who *built* the tree house?"

"I did, sir."

"Hmm." Mr. Wilsenholm leaned forward and plucked a cookie from the pretty plate on the table. "I was in your tree house, or I guess I should say *my* tree house yesterday. I looked it over pretty good. I must say I was impressed with the sturdiness of the construction. Where'd you get the materials for it?"

"Well, sir," Seth gulped, "I got them from a *few* places. The woodshop teacher gave me some of them . . . scraps and stuff, you know, that he was going to throw in the trash. The physical-education teacher gave me the rope 'cause it was too coarse for climbing; it was making too many blisters on kids' hands. My dad works . . . *worked* at the hardware store, and some scraps he brought home, you know, for kindling."

"Your dad teach you how to build like that?"

"Not really. I just sort of learned it on my own. I like working with wood."

Sara smiled. The conversation was beginning to feel more comfortable.

"My dad's really a farmer. At least that's what he has mostly done. But he could teach me to build, I mean, if I wanted him to. He's real good at all of that. I mean, he can do about *anything.*"

"Well, son, I wanted to meet the person who did such good work on that tree house. My ranch foreman is getting ready to retire. His kids are grown and he's tired of working, I guess. He says he'll stay on until I find someone to replace him, but he's not willing to work so hard anymore. I thought he might be able to use someone like you to help out. He could show you what he needs, for a while, that is, until I find a foreman to replace him."

An idea exploded in Seth's mind—and the exact idea exploded in Sara's mind at the same time. They looked at each other, knowing exactly what the other was thinking.

And then Mrs. Wilsenholm spoke.

"Stuart, maybe you could hire the boy's father. Seems like *he's* just the one you've been looking for."

Mr. Wilsenholm was very quiet for a long while . . . Sara and Seth sat silent . . . it seemed as though neither of them was even breathing. Then

Mr. Wilsenholm said, "You say your dad works at the hardware store?"

"Yes, sir."

"Tall man? Slender? Hair the color of yours?"

"Yes, sir."

"I believe I met him the other day. He helped me out of a real jam. Stayed after hours, too. Didn't complain a bit."

Sara and Seth looked at each other in amazement. They could barely believe that Mrs. Wilsenholm had actually spoken what they were thinking. This was all moving so fast.

"Did you say your father is looking for work?"

"Yes, sir. I mean, I *think* so."

Mr. Wilsenholm pulled his wallet from his pocket and took something out of it. He handed it to Seth.

"You give my card to your father. Ask him to give me a call if he's interested in managing my ranch. Tell him I'd like to talk with him about it. Might be a place for you, too, Seth, if ya want."

Mrs. Wilsenholm stood in the doorway. She was beaming with joy.

"Yes, sir," Seth blurted, looking at the business card like it was a shining piece of gold. "I'll give it to him right away."

Sara reached for a paper napkin Mrs. Wilsenholm had placed on the table in front of her. She hadn't realized it, but the little chocolate bits in her cookie had melted all over her hand. She stuffed what was left of the cookie in her mouth and nearly swallowed it whole while she wiped her hands on the napkin.

"Well, kids," said Mr. Wilsenholm, "thank you for stopping by. Sara, thank you for helping Mrs. Wilsenholm. And Seth, I'll look forward to hearing from your father. And if you kids want to play in *my* tree house, well, I guess that'd be all right with me. But you be careful now, you hear?"

Sara and Seth stood outside on the porch. They didn't know whether to laugh or cry or scream. They did their best to contain themselves as they faked calmness almost all the way to the end of the lane, and then they jumped in the air and "yippeed" for the next block and a half.

"No one would ever believe what just happened, Sara. We did it! We did it! We did it!"

CHAPTER 34

No Matter What

"**A**nd what in the Sam Hill makes him think that I'd be the least bit interested in working for him on that backbreaking ranch?" Seth's father snapped at Seth as he threw Mr. Wilsenholm's card down on the table.

Seth stood stunned at his father's response to what he'd believed was miraculous good news.

"What in hell were you doing over there in the *first* place?"

Seth stood quiet. He knew he'd never be able to explain to his father the long list of miracles—that the *Law of Attraction* had provided—that culminated in his meeting with Mr. Wilsenholm. Seth had learned from many past experiences that when his father was in one of these moods, it was better to just be quiet. The less said, the better. His father seemed to have a way of twisting every good intention into some act of wrongdoing.

Seth felt his eyes filling with tears. How could this be happening? How could something so wonderful be turning into something so awful? Was it really possible that his father was going to let this opportunity go by?

"Go on, get out of here!" his father yelled at Seth.

Seth was happy to get out of there before his father could see the tears in his eyes.

He washed his face, combed his hair, ducked out the front door, and ran all the way to school. He cut through the football field, slipped into the boys' locker room, came up the stairs into the gymnasium, climbed up high into the bleachers, and waited for the bell to ring. He didn't want to run into Sara this morning. He just couldn't bring himself to tell her the horrible news.

No point in spoiling her day, too, Seth thought.

Sara watched for Seth all day long. She could hardly wait to find out what had happened. She just knew his father would be thrilled to have this opportunity for such a wonderful job. The last bell rang. Sara wondered why she hadn't seen Seth yet, but she was so happy to be allowed back in the tree house that she gave little attention to her concern.

Seth was already perched up in the tree house when Sara arrived. She climbed happily up the ladder, but with her first look at Seth's face, she knew something was very wrong.

"What happened?" she asked.

"My dad doesn't want the job."

"*What?*" Sara blurted. She couldn't believe what she was hearing. Sara felt angry. "How can he . . . ?"

Solomon swooped in from above. *Well, good afternoon, my fine featherless friends.*

"Hi, Solomon," Sara mumbled. Seth didn't look up.

This is a very important part of the unfolding.

"*What* unfolding?" Seth said, angrily. "It isn't unfolding. It closed shut. My dad took care of that."

Well, I wouldn't be so sure about that if I were you.

"Why? Do you know something that we don't know?" Sara asked, hopefully.

Well, I know how the <u>Law of Attraction</u> works. And I know that you still have your vision to focus on. And I know that if you continue to focus on your version of the scenario—from your place of feeling good—the <u>Law of Attraction</u> can continue to assist you.

"But Solomon, my dad says he doesn't want the job."

I know how it looks, but the <u>Law of Attraction</u> is a powerful thing. Your father is a very proud man, Seth. And he had a strong reaction to this offer, from a place of feeling rejected by Mr. Bergheim. But you mustn't let *the current reality make you lose your place of connection. Remember, your power of influence depends on your staying connected to the Stream.*

I realize that it is always easier to stay connected to the Stream under good conditions, but the most masterful creators remain connected to the Stream, no matter what. That's what makes them masterful creators.

You see, kids, there are fair-weather creators and all-weather creators. It's easy to be a fair-weather creator, being happy when everything is just the way you like it, but when you are able to hold your vibration and feel good under all conditions—that is when your true creative ability shows.

And besides, your vision and the <u>Law of Attraction</u> have brought you such a long way already! I wouldn't give up the vision too soon.

Sara was feeling much better. Solomon had talked her through many a crisis. Seth looked brighter, too.

"Well, what should I say to my dad?"

Oh, I wouldn't say much of anything to him. Not about this, anyway, Solomon said. *I would just keep holding the vision of the happy outcome—and let the <u>Law of Attraction</u> figure out how to bring it about. You worry too much, my friend, when, in truth, there is nothing at all to worry about. Have faith in a happy outcome.*

"It's just that when my dad makes up his mind . . ."

Seth stopped in the middle of his sentence, aware that he was adding to the vibration of what he did *not* want.

Solomon smiled.

You see, Seth, that's what faith is: holding a vision of what is really wanted, even when the evidence points otherwise. Faith is about trusting the <u>Law of Attraction</u> and being willing to be patient while it does its work.

"I sure hope it hurries up."

Be patient—while the <u>Law of Attraction</u> does its work, Solomon repeated.

Seth and Sara laughed.

"Okay, Solomon. I'll work on this."

If I were standing in your shoes, I would bask in appreciation of standing here in this tree house. I would acknowledge how well things are working out for you. I would remember that one day you were banished from this glorious nest, and the next day you are the proud possessors of an unlimited access permit. That is an amazing thing. Do you agree?

"Yes," they answered at the same time.

I would take note of how powerful you are, and how the Universe lined up a sequence of perfect circumstances and events to assist you—and then I would take note that this stream of circumstances and events never ends. Good things will eternally flow to you. Keep an eye out for evidence of that.

You see, at one time, before so many wonderful things had happened, you had to make them up in your mind. But now you have the benefit of being able to remember those things while you continue to make more good things up in your mind. That's why it gets easier and easier. Have fun with all of this.

And with those last powerful words, Solomon flew up and away.

"That's one optimistic bird," Seth said and laughed, as Solomon flew away.

Sara laughed. "I want to be just like him."

"Yeah," Seth said. "Me, too."

Chapter 35
It's Nap Time?

Sara hadn't seen Seth at school all day; she couldn't believe that their paths hadn't crossed. She wanted to see him so that she could cheer him up if he needed it. She knew he was having a hard time holding himself in a good place with so much negative stuff going on at home.

And then she thought about what Solomon had been teaching them about ignoring *what is* if it doesn't please you and putting your attention on your dream or vision instead. She and Seth had been practicing it often, but Sara knew that *she* was a long way from being able to always control her thoughts, and she didn't know how Seth was managing it when he was living right in the middle of it all.

Sara thought about what a good friend Seth had become, and for a moment she felt a big, awful knot in her stomach as she imagined Seth no longer living in her mountain town. The feeling of emptiness was so severe it almost took her breath away.

"Whew!" Sara said out loud. "I guess it's clear that this thought doesn't match my desire."

Sara breathed deeply and tried to find a better-feeling thought. Her mind went immediately to the tree house, and to swinging on the big rope Seth had tied so securely to the tree. Then she thought about the platform, and them having been banished from it all, and how wonderfully everything had turned around. She thought of sweet Mrs. Wilsenholm and her kitten, and gruff Mr. Wilsenholm and the twinkle in his eye.

She thought of dear, sweet Solomon and the loving guidance that he always offered. She remembered how, when Solomon died, she believed her heart would break . . . how, when the worst thing imaginable happened, she had still survived, and how, in so many ways, things actually got better from that point. That point that seemed to be the absolute end of joy turned out instead to be the beginning point for so much *more* joy.

A flock of geese honked as they flew overhead, and Sara smiled as she remembered Solomon's earliest teachings about birds of a feather flocking together. And that reminded her of her very first introduction to the idea of the *Law of Attraction*.

"Boy, have we come a long way." She chuckled.

Sara noticed how—in just a few minutes of deliberately choosing her thoughts—that awful feeling in her stomach had lifted. She grinned as she realized that she was doing exactly what Solomon had taught them: She was setting her own tone.

"I'll wait two more minutes and if I don't see Seth, I'll go on to the tree house. He may not have come to school at all today. He'll probably just meet me there."

Two minutes passed and she headed for the tree house.

As Sara walked, her concern began to rise again. Hoping that Seth would be at the tree house but not knowing for sure only reminded Sara how important it was to her that he'd be there.

Well, even if he isn't there, that wouldn't mean anything. There are millions of things that could keep him from attending school or from coming to the tree house. That doesn't make any difference, she pretended. But her fear didn't change at all. In fact, if anything, it got worse.

The more Sara struggled to release the idea of Seth's moving away, the worse she felt. "This is ridiculous," Sara said out loud. "I certainly can control the way I feel."

I need a rampage of appreciation. (Sara remembered Solomon's game.) *Let's see, let me think of some things I appreciate:*

I appreciate how the <u>Law of Attraction</u> works for me, and for everyone.

I appreciate how Mrs. Wilsenholm helped us get our tree house back.

I appreciate how Mrs. Wilsenholm's cat introduced me to Mrs. Wilsenholm.

I appreciate how Mrs. Wilsenholm introduced us to Mr. Wilsenholm.

I appreciate knowing Seth. . . . Every time she thought about Seth, that sad, sick feeling rose up in Sara's stomach again. A tear rolled down her cheek. "Oh, Solomon," she whispered, "what will I do if Seth moves away? How will I *ever* find another friend like him?"

Sara wiped her face on her sleeve and was mad at herself for giving in to her sadness. "This isn't helping *anybody*," she said out loud.

Solomon's words were piling up in her mind: *Set your own tone . . . pay no attention to what-is . . . hold your attention on a happy outcome . . . the <u>Law of Attraction</u> will do the work . . . don't take score too soon . . . be easy about this . . . all is well here.* Those words helped.

Sara climbed up into the tree house, but Seth wasn't there. Solomon wasn't there either.

"Where *are* you guys?" Sara said out loud.

Sara tried to find happy thoughts, but the *now* reality, and the absence of Seth, were too strong for her to overcome.

A nice long nap is a good idea, Solomon said, dropping down from above to the floor of the tree house.

"*Solomon!* Where have you been?"

Everywhere. Solomon smiled.

"Solomon—" Sara began.

Solomon interrupted. *Sara, sometimes the best thing to do is to get your mind off of whatever it is you are worrying about. The <u>Law of Attraction</u> is taking care of things. Go home, sweet girl, and go to bed early.*

Solomon flew up to the branch where the big rope was tied and then lifted up and out of Sara's view.

"Geez, even Solomon can't cheer me up," Sara whined.

She climbed down the ladder and went home.

"I need a nap."

CHAPTER 36

Remember Your Vision

This had been the first day since moving to Sara's town that Seth hadn't been at school. He had awakened to the sound of his mother bringing boxes into the living room, setting them all around the room in readiness for packing.

"What are all these boxes for?" Seth asked, knowing very well what they were for. He stepped over them and around them, trying to make his way into the kitchen.

"For packing. We're moving on," his mother said quietly. Seth could hear the disappointment in her voice. Although his mother didn't have much to say about anything, Seth sensed that she had come to really like this little mountain town; she had seemed more content than Seth had ever seen before. And while she always stayed busy and worked harder than Seth thought she needed to, this stay, in this house, with her husband making good money at the hardware store, had been a big relief from the hardworking farm life that she'd been used to.

Seth felt sad as he watched his mother. He could feel her dreading the unknown future. (Or maybe it wasn't as unknown to her as Seth thought.)

"Start saying good-bye, son. Most likely we won't be here more than another week or so."

Seth felt a big lump forming in his throat. "Yeah," he said, going out on the porch.

"Solomon," Seth said softly, under his breath.

Remember your vision. Seth heard Solomon's voice in his head.

Holding on to the porch post, Seth closed his eyes and *saw* himself swinging on the long rope at the tree house. In his mind, he could *hear* Sara's laugh, and he could *feel* the wind on his face. The lump dissolved. He instantly felt better.

Take it further. He heard Solomon's voice again. *See your mother.*

Seth kept his eyes closed tightly. He *imagined* his mother working happily around the house; he *imagined* her feeling relief. She was smiling. He instantly felt relief.

This is good work. Seth heard Solomon's voice in his head.

Seth opened his eyes. He could hear his mother moving boxes about, but he struggled to hold his attention on something else, anything else. He didn't want to go back to the painful reality. He wanted to hold his attention on his own chosen vision.

"I don't know where you've been spending your time, son, but wherever it is, you best go spend some time there now. While ya can."

Was his mother actually encouraging him to go to the tree house? It seemed so.

Seth bolted off the front porch and ran down Thacker's Trail. Up, up, up into his glorious tree he climbed. Breathless, he sat there alone and exhilarated.

Good things will eternally flow to you. Keep an eye out for evidence of that. Seth remembered Solomon's words.

He smiled. His mother had just given him evidence that well-being was flowing.

Seth closed his eyes, and from his place of connection he imagined good things: He *pretended* that his father was happy. He didn't try to figure out *why* he was happy. Only that he was happy. He *mentally* saw his mother smiling. He *saw* Sara smiling. That was easy.

Seth took hold of his swinging rope, and with eyes closed he leaped from the tree, swinging back and forth with the wind in his face, feeling his flight, and knowing—at least for this brief moment—that all was truly well.

CHAPTER 37

Well-being Abounds

Hearing the cow bells on the front door clanking, indicating that someone had come inside, Seth's father came out from the back room at the hardware store.

"Can I help you with something?"

"Need some longer screws that'll fit these cabinet knobs. Knobs keep pulling off of these short screws."

"They'd be over here, then. Let's see, I believe these would be the ones. Here. Try this one."

The old man fumbled with the screw and the knob, making sure that it was the right fit. "Well, I believe you're right. Thank you, sir. You made this an easy job for me. I'll need 24 of them. Better make it 30 in case I drop some in the straw. They're for the cupboards in the horse barn, and the straw's deep in there. My clumsy old fingers are likely to throw a few of them in the straw."

Seth's dad laughed. This was a likable man. "Oh, I wouldn't worry about that. Looks to me like you're doing just fine."

"Well, I'll be doing finer before long. I'm retirin'. Me and the missus are going to travel. I've been promisin' to take her to visit her family back east for years. Now we're finally going to do it. Never felt like I could take the time away, ya know. But now I'm ready. And she sure is ready, too. Patient woman. Sure enough."

"What's been keeping you so busy that you couldn't get away?"

"Been foreman at the Wilsenholm ranch for years. Been a good job, too. Got no complaints. Pays well. Got plenty of reliable men who do a good job. Gotta keep yer eye on 'em, you know what I mean? But they're a hardworking bunch, and honest enough. Boss says he really hates to see me go. Says I been making the place run for years, but he feels real good about a lead he has on a man to replace me. Says he met the man and feels real good about what he's seen. And he says he's got the best recommendation that anyone would need: a recommendation from the man's own son. Well, I'd better get goin'. Wife gets unhappy if she has to keep supper waiting on me. Thanks for yer help."

Seth's dad stood silent. It was as if a giant weight had lifted from him. He pulled the folded card from his pocket and reached for the telephone. . . .

At that very same moment at the swinging tree, thrilling goosebumps popped up all over Seth's body. He opened his eyes, realizing that the rope had stopped swinging and he was hanging dead center in the middle of the stream. "Boy, I'm getting carried away with this dreaming stuff." He dropped into the water and waded back up onto the riverbank. . . .

Well-being abounds. He heard Solomon's voice in his head. *Well-being abounds.*

CHAPTER 38

We Did It!

Sara awakened, feeling much better! The awful sensation had passed in the night, and as she walked down the front steps, she felt renewed and invigorated.

This is a beautiful day, Sara thought as she began her walk to school.

Looking up ahead, she could see someone standing right out in the middle of the intersection. Sara smiled broadly as she realized that it was Seth. When he spotted Sara, he began running toward her.

Sara couldn't make out his words, as he was running and calling, but whatever he was saying was obviously *good* news. He was half running, half leaping, and smiling—and yelling.

And then Sara began to hear his words.

"Sara, you won't believe it, you won't *believe* it! He's taking the job! He's *taking* the job! *He's taking the job!* We can stay, Sara. It's a miracle. Solomon was right, Sara! *We did it! We did it!*"

Sara dropped her book bag at the roadside, and she and Seth locked forearms and jumped up and down together, shouting, *"We did it! We did it! We did it!"*

A neighbor backed out of his driveway and drove slowly past them, gawking with amused interest at their joyous roadside display.

They laughed. "Guess we look a little weird," Seth said.

"If they only knew," Sara laughed. "If they only knew!"

Honk, honk. The geese honked from overhead.

Sara and Seth looked up. A magnificent flock of geese was flying by in a perfect V formation, and who was bringing up the rear, but Solomon.

Seth and Sara squealed in delight.

Solomon broke formation and spiraled down to Sara and Seth.

"Solomon, what in the world are you doing flocking with geese?"

Well, most would find that more likely than my flocking with you, Sara and Seth, my fine featherless friends.

Sara and Seth laughed.

I've always wondered what that would be like.

"What, Solomon?"

Flying in formation. Owls don't do that, you know.

They laughed again.

Well, see ya, Solomon said, lifting up into the sky. *I've got a lot of practicing to do. They're very strict, you know. These geese, they like precision.*

"See ya, Solomon. Meet you in our tree house?"

I'll be there, Solomon called back. *I'll be there. . . .*

THE BEGINNING

About the Authors

Excited about the clarity and practicality of the translated word from the Beings who call themselves Abraham, **Esther** and **Jerry Hicks** began disclosing their amazing Abraham experience to a handful of close business associates in 1986.

Recognizing the practical results being received by themselves and by those people who were asking practical questions and then applying Abraham's answers to their own situations, Esther and Jerry made a deliberate decision to allow the teachings of Abraham to become available to an ever-widening circle of seekers of how to live a happier life.

Using their San Antonio, Texas, conference center as their base, Jerry and Esther have traveled to approximately 50 cities a year since 1989, presenting interactive *Law of Attraction* workshops to those leaders who gather to participate in this expanding stream of progressive thought. And although worldwide attention has been given to this philosophy of Well-Being by Leading Edge thinkers and teachers who have, in turn, incorporated many of Abraham's *Law of Attraction* concepts into their best-selling books, scripts, lectures, and so forth, the primary spread of this material has been from person to person—as individuals begin to discover the value of this form of spiritual practicality in their personal life experiences.

In November 2011, Jerry made his transition into Non-Physical, and now Esther continues to conduct the Abraham workshops with the help of her physical friends and co-workers and, of course, with the Non-Physical help of Abraham and Jerry.

People are able to access Abraham directly by attending the seminars in person or by participating in the online live streaming of most events. There is also an extensive YouTube library of Abraham videos.

Abraham—a group of uplifting Non-Physical teachers—present their Broader Perspective through Esther Hicks. And as they speak to our level of comprehension through a series of loving, allowing, brilliant, yet comprehensively simple essays in print and in sound, they guide us to a clear connection with our loving *Inner Being,* and to uplifting self-empowerment from our Total Self.

Abraham-Hicks Publications may be contacted through the extensive interactive website: **www. abraham-hicks.com**; or by mail at Abraham-Hicks Publications, P.O. Box 690070, San Antonio, TX 78269.

We hope you enjoyed this Hay House book. If you'd like to receive our online catalog featuring additional information on Hay House books and products, or if you'd like to find out more about the Hay Foundation, please contact:

Hay House, Inc., P.O. Box 5100, Carlsbad, CA 92018-5100
(760) 431-7695 or (800) 654-5126
(760) 431-6948 (fax) or (800) 650-5115 (fax)
www.hayhouse.com® • www.hayfoundation.org

———

Published in Australia by: Hay House Australia Pty. Ltd.,
18/36 Ralph St., Alexandria NSW 2015
Phone: 612-9669-4299 • *Fax:* 612-9669-4144
www.hayhouse.com.au

Published in the United Kingdom by: Hay House UK, Ltd.,
The Sixth Floor, Watson House, 54 Baker Street, London W1U 7BU
Phone: +44 (0)20 3927 7290 • *Fax:* +44 (0)20 3927 7291
www.hayhouse.co.uk

Published in India by: Hay House Publishers India,
Muskaan Complex, Plot No. 3, B-2, Vasant Kunj, New Delhi 110 070
Phone: 91-11-4176-1620 • *Fax:* 91-11-4176-1630
www.hayhouse.co.in

———

Access New Knowledge.
Anytime. Anywhere.

Learn and evolve at your own pace
with the world's leading experts.

www.hayhouseU.com

Listen. Learn. Transform.

Listen to the audio version of this book for FREE!

Today, life is more hectic than ever—so you deserve on-demand and on-the-go solutions that inspire growth, center your mind, and support your well-being.

Introducing the *Hay House Unlimited Audio* mobile app. Now you can listen to this book (and countless others)—without having to restructure your day.

With your membership, you can:

- Enjoy over 30,000 hours of audio from your favorite authors.
- Explore audiobooks, meditations, Hay House Radio episodes, podcasts, and more.
- Listen anytime and anywhere with offline listening.
- Access exclusive audios you won't find anywhere else.

Try FREE for 7 days!

Visit hayhouse.com/unlimited to start your free trial and get one step closer to living your best life.